Yesterday and Today in the U.S.A.

Intermediate ESL Reader

SECOND EDITION

Anna Harris Live

formerly, Director, English Program for Foreign Students
University of Pennsylvania

PRENTICE HALL, ENGLEWOOD CLIFFS, NEW JERSEY 07632

LIBRARY OF CONGRESS
Library of Congress Cataloging-in-Publication Data

Live, Anna Harris
    Yesterday and today in the U.S.A. : intermediate ESL reader / Anna
Harris Live. -- 2nd ed.
      p.   cm.
    ISBN 0-13-971888-5
    1. Readers--United States. 2. Readers--History. 3. English
language--Textbooks for foreign speakers. 4. United States-
-Civilization.   I. Title.
PE1127.H5L58 1988
428.2'4--dc19   87-37691
                                                              CIP

*Editorial/production supervision and
    interior design:* Alison D. Gnerre
Cover design: Diane Saxe
Manufacturing buyer: Margaret Rizzi

Cover photos: *Top left*, Library of Congress, photo by E. Levick; *top right*, Robert E. Mates; *bottom left*, Library of Congress; *bottom center*, Ken Karp; *bottom right*, Courtesy of the Rice Council.

To I., T., and D.

 © 1988 by Prentice-Hall, Inc.
A Division of Simon & Schuster
Englewood Cliffs, New Jersey 07632

Printed in the United States of America

10 9 8 7 6 5 4 3 2 1

ISBN 0-13-971888-5

Prentice-Hall International (UK) Limited, *London*
Prentice-Hall of Australia Pty. Limited, *Sydney*
Prentice-Hall Canada Inc., *Toronto*
Prentice-Hall Hispanoamericana, S.A., *Mexico*
Prentice-Hall of India Private Limited, *New Delhi*
Prentice-Hall of Japan, Inc., *Tokyo*
Prentice-Hall of Southeast Asia Pte. Ltd., *Singapore*
Editora Prentice-Hall do Brasil, Ltda., *Rio de Janeiro*

Contents

Preface

The function of this book is to enhance the English proficiency of non-native speakers, while at the same time introducing them to some distinctive aspects of the American background. This approach serves the purpose of helping to adapt them both to the language and to the environment.

Members of relatively isolated other-language ''ethnic communities'' often need such twofold help, as do students from abroad, even when equipped with some school-acquired English. Both groups need to attain a meaningful grasp of the structure of English and an awareness of its special traits. To this end, rules or generalizations are here stated simply and economically, and are illustrated with examples drawn from the readings. This language material is designed so as to help students to apply what they have learned to their own speech and writing. In addition, turns-of-phrase and idioms as well as vocabulary are presented in such a manner as to alert students to connotations and to considerations of the situational appropriateness of a word, a pattern, or a particular expression. Accordingly, paraphrases are presented with indication of the style level of each alternative. Examples of such paraphrasing are given here with each selection, and the teacher can readily supplement these with further illustrations and with examples of appropriate contexts.

A short vocabulary list precedes the selection to suggest prior consideration of those words, so as to make the reading (or aural) comprehension go more smoothly; and a number of short language lessons of various types follow it. These include supplementary vocabulary study, with attention to synonyms and the distinctions of meaning among them, and other semantic considerations; pronunciation; morphology; grammatical patterns and idioms. There is also a spelling lesson, emphasizing the regularities of English orthography and pointing out exceptions. Each of these various explanations and drills focuses on a problem which is likely to trouble these students, and all are based on occurrences within the accompanying selection. In addition there are questions on its subject matter as well as more general suggestive questions to stimulate discussion.

Grammatical and other explanations have been kept to a minimum. The teacher's guide gives fuller clarification as well as the rationale for the particular lesson, and suggestions for further expansions.

There is also a glossary of peculiarly American terms, each with a very brief explanation (e.g., *pony express, wetback, Confederacy, Uncle Tom, dust bowl*). These are chosen as significant expressions reflecting concepts and situations of American life, past and present.

The reading selections advance progressively in difficulty and in length. They do not deal with wars, politics, or the other usual topics of schoolbook history. Their subject matter is selected from phases of our background that are distinctly American, events and phenomena of human and cultural interest that have left their stamp on American life. Such material as well as the glossary terms would be meaningful and revealing to students from non-American home environments in facilitating their comprehension and interpretation of what they observe (including allusions that would otherwise baffle them), thus helping them to overcome their cultural isolation.

In this new edition exercises have been incorporated in each chapter so as to give students an opportunity to practice the newly-learned item immediately after having studied the explanation (with its illustrations). These should be useful to the teacher, too: he/she could readily expand an exercise, along the same lines, if the class seems to need further review. Following the reading and the language-learning sections, the speaking-and-writing section focuses on the *productive* use of English. The reading selections have been updated where pertinent, to make the information current.

The book starts out at the lower intermediate level and advances to a considerably higher one. Moreover, the manner of instruction can adapt the material to a wide range of student-proficiency levels and of ages. By varying the degree of preliminary preparation and help given in anticipation of each selection, the teacher can adjust the lesson to the needs of the students. Further flexibility is available through the choice of language materials; the teacher may use all of the accompanying lessons or cull out the pertinent ones from among them, as the occasion demands. Oral presentation of a new selection (without the student's recourse to the text) is another useful variant. Also, particularly for younger students, many of the situations presented in the readings lend themselves to dramatization or role-playing, while older pupils and the foreign-born students can readily be stimulated to discuss or debate some of the issues involved, as suggested by the ''discussion questions.''

Thus the material offered can be adapted and tailored to the needs of various groups of foreign students and Americans for whom English is a second language. It should substantially develop their command of the language, and incidentally their understanding of some phases of the American experience. If this leads to a more responsive attitude toward the United States, so much the better.

I should like to express profound gratitude to my wise and generous sister, Suzanne Harris Sankowsky, for her help and guidance, especially in her fields of history and sociology.

Note on Pronunciation Symbols

In designating symbols for English sounds I intentionally avoid both a consistent phonemic system and a precise phonetic one. The use of either would involve considerable expenditure of time in attaining familiarity with the system itself, time better expended on learning English. Instead I use symbols pedagogically suited to differentiating those sounds which the student must perceive and utter as distinctively different. In designating vowel sounds I include the glide symbols [y] or [w] to emphasize the diphthongal pronunciation of the so-called "long **a**" (*say*) and "long **o**" (*sew*), since many foreigners tend to miss the glide; likewise to signal the glide (or length) in "long **e**" (*see*) and "long **u**" (*sue*); thus [sey], [sow], [siy], [suw], respectively. To differentiate the vowels of *put* and *but* from the [uw] sound as well as from the student's native [u] I indicate them by [U] and [ʌ], respectively, so that *put* is [pUt] and *but* is [bʌt]. For the "short **i**" (*pit*) I use [I] to avoid confusion with the higher, more fronted vowel associated with the letter **i** in many languages and represented here by [i]. Analogously I use [ɛ] for "short **e**" (*pet*); [a] is for the **a** of *car* and the **o** of *cot*, and [æ] for *cat*. The [ɔ] symbol is used for "open **o**" (*more, long, law, because*), and [ə] for the schwa sound which occurs so frequently in unstressed syllables in English. Most of the consonantal sounds have their regular alphabetic designations, but [č] represents what is usually spelled **ch** and [š] represents the usual **sh**; [θ] is voiceless **th** (*thin*), and [ð] is the voiced counterpart (*this*); also [ŋ] represents the sound of final *ng*, and [ž], the sound spelled *s* in *vision, pleasure*.

1

The First Americans

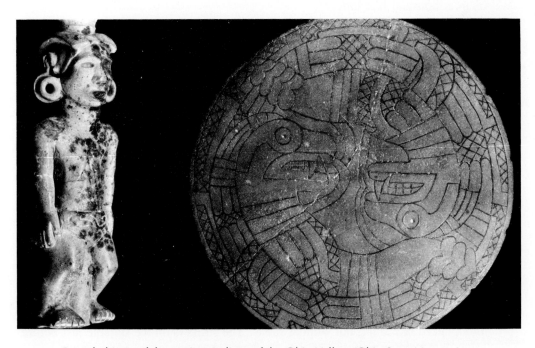

Carved objects of the ancient Indians of the Ohio Valley. (Ohio State Museum)

strait	strange
migration	shape
remain	mound
village	form
adobe	culture
develop	evolve
carved object	

More than twelve thousand years ago the first American Indians came to Alaska from Asia by crossing the Bering land bridge, which later became the Bering Strait. This slow migration went on for thousands of years. From Alaska the Indians traveled on southward. Some of them remained in North America, while others kept on moving farther south—to Central and South America. After 5 many centuries they learned how to grow corn, which they had found as a wild plant. Later, about 1000 A.D., some of the Indians of what is now southwestern United States began to live in villages in houses of adobe, a sun-baked clay.

About 300 A.D. the Indians in the Ohio River region developed a high level of civilization. In addition to beautiful carved objects, they have left strange- 10 ly shaped mounds of earth over their burial places. These man-made hills were formed in the shapes of animals. The largest is the Great Serpent Mound, more than a thousand feet long.

Higher civilizations were developed by the Maya and the Aztec Indians in Mexico, and the Incas in Peru. Many different cultures evolved among the Indian 15 tribes long before Europeans came to America.

A. PRONUNCIATION

The sound [j] can be pronounced as [dž] or as voiced [č] (see Note on Pronunciation Symbols).

bridge	strange	Jim, gym
village	ginger	job
region	Georgia	jet
large	June	Jamaica

B. WORD FORMATION

The noun ending **-tion**, added to many verbs, forms a related noun: The ending is pronounced like *shun*, but without stress. The stress is on the syllable just before **-tion**.

NOUN	VERB
migration	migrate
civilization	civilize
addition	add
correction	correct
relation	relate

C. GRAMMAR

Answering "how" questions.

1. How did the Indians come?
   —by crossing the Bering land bridge.
   They came by crossing the Bering land bridge.
2. How did they reach South America?
   —by moving south.
3. How did they find corn growing?
   —as a wild plant.
4. How did the Pueblo Indians of the Southwest live?
   —in villages.
5. How did you draw the picture?
   —with a crayon.

PRACTICE EXERCISE

Make up answers (both in the short form and in the full sentence) to each of these questions.

Examples:

How did the Indians of the Southwest build their houses?
   —of adobe. (short form)
      They built their houses of adobe.
How do you go to school?
   —by bus.
      I go to school by bus.

1. How did you come to this city?
2. How did he earn the money?
3. How do you practice speaking English?
4. How did you meet your friend?

5. How did Mary find her gloves?
6. How did you break the glass?
7. How did Jim get to the airport?

D. SPELLING

The final (silent) **e** is lost before an ending which begins with a vowel.

	+ ed	+ ing	+ able
move	moved	moving	movable
live	lived	living	livable
shape	shaped	shaping	
carve	carved	carving	
evolve	evolved	evolving	
save	saved	saving	
like	liked	liking	likable

PRACTICE EXERCISE

Add the suffixes -**ed** and -**ing** to each of the following words: care, wake, phone, chase, combine, dance, waste, move, hope.

E. PARAPHRASE

FORMAL (*as in lectures or in books, etc.*)	COLLOQUIAL (*as in informal talk*)
1. were formed in the shapes of animals	1. were made to look like animals
2. strangely shaped mounds of earth	2. funny little hills
3. many years ago	3. way back

F. IDIOMS

12,000 years ago = 12,000 years before the present
kept on moving = continued to move
went on = was in progress

G. SEMANTICS

Note the difference between these closely related words:

> A **mound** is a small pile of earth, often made by man.
> A **hill** is not very high.
> A **mountain** is very high.

PRACTICE EXERCISE

Complete these sentences with one of the following words: *mound, hill, mountain.*

1. We walked up to the top of the _____; it was an easy walk.

2. The child piled the sand up into a _____.

3. Hilary became famous because he climbed the highest _____.

4. The _____ is green, but the _____ is so high that its top is always white with snow.

H. COMPREHENSION

1. Where did the American Indians come from?
2. How did they learn about corn?
3. What did the Indians who lived near the Ohio River leave?
4. Which Indians developed the highest cultures?

I. SPEAKING AND WRITING

Discussion

1. Can you guess what happened to the land bridge that the Indians crossed?
2. What foods are made from corn?

3. Why did the American Indians think that corn was a gift of the gods?
4. Adobe is used for houses in many hot, dry countries. Why?

Summary (main idea)

What did you learn about the early Indians? Answer in one or two sentences.

2

Thanksgiving

"Starting Life Anew in the Wilderness," a painting by Clyde DeLand, showing Pilgrims building their first shelter. (Philadelphia Board of Education)

Pilgrims	fall
voyage	harvest
hardship	turkey
seed	celebrate
crop	invite

The Pilgrims left their home in England in search of religious freedom. After a long, hard voyage across the Atlantic Ocean, their ship, the *Mayflower*, finally reached land. In November, 1620, the Pilgrims sailed into Cape Cod Bay in Massachusetts to start their new life. Their first winter was full of hardship. In the spring they planted seeds, and all summer long they worked on their farms and prayed for good crops. When fall came, they had a very good harvest with plenty of food for the winter. In addition, the men went hunting in the woods and shot wild turkeys. The Pilgrims were very thankful. They prepared a great feast and invited their friendly Indian neighbors to enjoy it with them. 5

In memory of that happy occasion Americans celebrate Thanksgiving 10
Day every year. They invite relatives and friends to eat turkey and other tasty foods and to give thanks for all good things.

A. PRONUNCIATION

1. **-ed**, the verb ending, is pronounced as a separate syllable only if it comes after the sound [d] or [t].

2 SYLLABLES	3 SYLLABLES
planted	invited
hunted	repeated
started	decided
faded	commanded
loaded	

2. **-ed** is pronounced [t] after other voiceless consonants (*p, k, sh, ch, s, f*); the **e** is not pronounced.

1 SYLLABLE

reached	looked	washed	fixed
worked	hoped	passed	

3. **-ed** is pronounced [d] in all other situations (that is, after voiced consonants and after vowels). Note that the **e** is not pronounced.

1 SYLLABLE	2 SYLLABLES
raised	prepared
sailed	arranged
named	enjoyed
urged	followed
begged	
prayed	

PRACTICE EXERCISE

How many syllables does each of these words have? (Do you pronounce the **-ed** as a separate syllable?)

Examples:

	Number of syllables
counted	2
stayed	1
avoided	3

mailed, celebrated, carved, lived, traveled, obeyed, developed, shaped, liked, corrected

B. WORD FORMATION

The ending **-ful** added to a noun changes the noun into an adjective.

thankful
  He felt thanks. = He was thankful.
hopeful
  This gives us hope. = This makes us hopeful.
harmful
  Overeating does harm to a person. = Overeating is harmful.

C. GRAMMAR

Certain verbs of request or command are followed by a noun or pronoun, then an infinitive. The noun or pronoun is the subject of the infinitive.

invited them to come
asked John to leave
ordered the driver to stop the car
begged him to help

D. SPELLING

In many words the spelling **ea** is pronounced [iy], just like **ee**.

sea	reach	see	feel
meat	hear	meet	tree
beat	seat	beet	bee
feast	meal	seed	
eat	bean	feet	

In some words **ea** before **r** and another consonant has the sound [ə].

search	pearl
earn	heard
learn	early

E. PARAPHRASE

FORMAL	COLLOQUIAL
1. in search of _____	1. trying to find _____
2. The harvest was excellent.	2. The crops were great.
3. They prepared a great feast.	3. They fixed a big spread.

F. IDIOMS

1. all summer long = throughout the summer
   all day long = throughout the day
   all week long
   all year long

PRACTICE EXERCISE

This idiom pattern is not used to describe shorter intervals like a minute or an hour, nor calendar dates. It emphasizes the long stretch of a period from beginning to end. Make up sentences using each of these expressions. If you prefer, you can substitute similar ones, like *all night long, all winter long, all month long.*

2. go hunting = hunt, engage in hunting
   go fishing
   go swimming
   go hiking

G. SEMANTICS

SYNONYMS

voyage—long, usually by sea
  After the voyage across the ocean, they were glad to be on land again.
trip—usually short, to a definite place
  We took a vacation trip to Canada.
journey—usually long, over land
  They packed their belongings for the journey.

feast—emphasis on food
  All the neighbors were invited to the lavish feast.
party—emphasis on fun
  Her parents gave a party for her birthday.

H. COMPREHENSION

1. What kind of crossing (voyage) did the Pilgrims have?
2. Where did they land?
3. Why did the Pilgrims celebrate?
4. Who came to the feast?
5. How do Americans remember this event?

I. SPEAKING AND WRITING

Discussion

1. How do you suppose the Pilgrims felt living in a strange new land?
2. As a place to live in, how was it different from their homeland?

3. Did they have special reasons to be thankful?
4. Do you have a harvest holiday in your native land? How is it celebrated?

Summary

Summarize the reading selection in your own words, in a sentence or two.

3

The New England Town Meeting

Counting the votes at a modern town meeting. (Jonathan D. Lynch)

assemble	community
discuss	property
express	common
opinion	widely imitated
official	current (*adjective*)
decision	policy

From their beginnings New England towns had a special democratic system of government. At stated times all the citizens would assemble at a town meeting, where they would discuss local problems and express opinions freely. They also elected the town's officials at these gatherings and made decisions about the taxes they would pay and about other community matters. These meet- 5 ings were usually held at the town hall, after such a building had been constructed in the central square.

In the eighteenth-century town meetings, only men who owned property and who were church members actually voted, although everyone present was allowed to express opinions. Later, all citizens were allowed to vote. Thus the 10 town meeting became truly democratic. Town meetings are still common in New England communities.

In recent years the town meeting idea has been widely imitated. There are open sessions of this kind on radio and television. Occasionally a meeting of this type is called by a government agency in order to give an opportunity for free and 15 open discussion on current problems and policies.

A. PRONUNCIATION

The sound [ŋ] at the end of a word (spelled **-ng**) is made farther back in the mouth than [n]. The **g** is not pronounced.

sing	going
rang	seeing
wrong	assembling
young	deciding

B. WORD FORMATION

Although it is usually a verb ending, **-ing** can also be a noun ending.

a meeting
a building
a gathering
an ending
a wedding
a christening

C. GRAMMAR

Would is used to express custom or habit in the past.

They would assemble every Monday.
They would discuss problems.
We would visit my grandmother on weekends.
I would practice for an hour after school.
They would go to church on Sunday.

D. SPELLING

Practice spelling words with double consonants.

common	beginning
community	discuss
opportunity	express
session	actually
discussion	usually
current	

E. PARAPHRASE

FORMAL	COLLOQUIAL
1. from the beginning	1. right off
2. They assembled at a meeting.	2. They got together.
3. after the building had been constructed	3. after they put up the building
4. gave him an opportunity to express his ideas	4. let him have his say

PRACTICE EXERCISE

Change each sentence, using the colloquial expression instead of the more formal one.

Example:

Before they voted, they gave him an opportunity to express his ideas.
Before they voted, they let him have his say.

1. I liked this job from the beginning.
2. They assembled at a meeting to discuss the problem.
3. After the building had been constructed, they met there.

F. IDIOMS

1. Special pairings of verb and object:

   made a decision
   held an opinion
   called a meeting
   held a meeting
2. at stated times = according to a regular schedule

G. SEMANTICS

Words related in meaning:

neighborhood—emphasis on the place
It is a pleasant neighborhood to live in.
community—emphasis on people
The community is interested in maintaining good schools.

PRACTICE EXERCISE

Fill in each blank.

Example:

The houses in our **neighborhood** are modern.

1. They live in a warm and friendly _____.

2. The residents of this _____ take good care of their gardens.

3. The frequent meetings of the citizens in this _____ help to keep it a close-knit _____ .

H. COMPREHENSION

1. Who attended the New England town meetings?
2. What did they talk about?
3. Why was the town meeting a good idea?
4. What town meetings are held nowadays?

I. SPEAKING AND WRITING

Discussion

1. Would a town meeting be useful in your town? Why?
2. Why do you suppose the oldest town meetings gave the vote only to property-owning church members?
3. What current problems could be handled well in a town meeting? Why?

Summary

In a sentence or two, tell what you learned about town meetings.

4

The Quakers, Then and Now

Interior of an early Quaker home. (Philip B. Wallace)

principle

pacifism

guide (*verb*)

convert (*noun*)

aristocrat

grant

deal (*verb*)

fair

humane

slave

humanitarian

The Society of Friends (commonly called Quakers) was founded on the principles of simple living and pacifism. Each member must be guided by his or her own "inner light" or "Christ within" rather than by the rules of a religious establishment. One of its early converts was a rich, aristocratic Englishman named William Penn. In 1681 he persuaded the King of England to grant him land for a Quaker colony in America, to be named Pennsylvania (meaning Penn's forest). Penn called his colony the "Holy Experiment" because of the ideals on which it was based, and he named its capital Philadelphia, city of brotherly love. He invited and welcomed to his colony settlers of various religions from different countries, and gave them free land. Penn also dealt fairly and honorably with the Indians, and the colony was on good terms with them.

Over the years Quakers have worked for many humane causes. Before the Civil War some of them actively opposed slavery and helped runaway slaves to escape. Today the Friends Service Committee carries on many humanitarian projects. The committee fights hunger and disease in parts of Africa as well as in Haiti and on American-Indian reservations. In African Mali and Senegal it helps villages to become economically independent by establishing irrigation systems, and in the Philippines it supplies water buffaloes to poor farmers to use in ploughing and planting and for transportation. The committee also helps the homeless in the United States. The Society of Friends truly lives up to its name.

A. PRONUNCIATION

-er is pronounced [ər].

Quak**er**

memb**er**

inn**er**

rath**er**

hung**er**

settl**er**

broth**er**

B. WORD FORMATION

The adverbial ending **-ly** tells "how."

ADJECTIVE	ADVERB
fair	fairly
honorable	honorably
slow	slowly
quick	quickly
great	greatly

PRACTICE EXERCISE

Change the wording of each sentence so that an adverb is used instead of the underlined adjective.

Examples:

They were active in opposing slavery.
　　They opposed slavery actively.

Her report of the event was fair.
　　She reported the event fairly.

1. He was glad to come.
2. She gave a different answer.
3. They led a simple life.
4. The pianist gave an excellent performance.
5. Jim is a slow worker.

C. GRAMMAR

Verbs of "naming" have two objects: the thing or person being named and the name given.

　　They called the city Philadelphia.
　　They named the colony Pennsylvania.
　　They labeled him a hero.

D. SPELLING

Don't confuse these words which sound alike:

principal (*adjective*) = most important
principal (*noun*) = head of a school
principle (*noun only*) = basic idea

capital = (a) money invested
            (b) the city of the government
Capitol = building where Congress meets

PRACTICE EXERCISE

Fill in each blank with the correct word (principal, principle, capital, Capitol).

1. Peace is one of the _____ of the Quakers.

2. Hunger is a _____ problem in Ethiopia.

3. The student asked the _____ to let her join that class.

4. The _____ has a round tower.

5. Washington is the _____ of the United States.

6. To establish such a business requires a great deal of _____.

E. PARAPHRASE

FORMAL	COLLOQUIAL
1. He persuaded the king to grant him land.	1. He got the king to give him land.
2. Penn dealt fairly and honorably.	2. He was fair and square.
3. helping them to become economically independent	3. putting them on their own feet.
4. according to the dictates of a religious establishment	4. by the rules of a church

F. IDIOMS

carry on = maintain
work for a cause = help in an effort for social good
over the years = as the years passed
on good terms = in friendly relation

G. SEMANTICS

Words related in meaning:

idea = thought
principle = basic idea, or idea that one believes in
rule = way of behavior which one must follow

H. COMPREHENSION

1. Explain the name Philadelphia.
2. How did Penn deal with his Indian neighbors?
3. Why did people from different places and of different religions come to Pennsylvania?
4. What do Quakers think about war?
5. What did some Quakers do about slavery?

I. SPEAKING AND WRITING

Discussion

1. Do you agree with the Quaker principles?
2. Do you know of any places where humanitarian help is needed?

Summary

What are the Quakers, and what do they do?

5

The Gifted
Dr. Franklin

Franklin, the scientist, experimenting with a kite and a key to test whether lightning is electric.

gifted	efficient
eager	heater
contribute	lightning rod
learned	earn
initiate	draw up
improvement	negotiate
pave	treaty
lighted street	Abolitionist

In 1723 there arrived in Philadelphia a penniless young man, eager for work and for knowledge. As the years passed, this man, Benjamin Franklin, contributed greatly to his city and to his country. He became a printer and a publisher, and a learned man in many subjects. He also helped to spread learning by establishing a public library and by founding the American Philosophical   5
Society, which is an important academy of great scholars to this day.

Franklin initiated many improvements in the city of Philadelphia, making it one of the world's first cities to have paved and lighted streets as well as a police force and a fire-fighting company. He was also an inventor. His many practical inventions included the Franklin stove, which was a very efficient heater, and the   10
lightning rod, which was used to protect buildings in electric storms. His scientific work with electricity earned Franklin world fame.

Franklin played an important role in the early history of the United States. He took part in drawing up the Declaration of Independence and the Constitution. He was the first ambassador to France, and he helped negotiate the Treaty of   15
1783, which ended the Revolutionary War.

As an active member and as president of the Abolitionist Society, Franklin devoted the last years of his life to the movement to end slavery.

A. PRONUNCIATION

Practice the sound [ər] before a consonant.

learn	first
earn	heard
bird	word
curl	world
burst	worst

B. WORD FORMATION

The noun suffix **-ment** is added to some verbs to form nouns.

VERB	NOUN
establish	establishment
improve	improvement
judge	judgment
assort	assortment

C. GRAMMAR

by ___ **ing** = through the act of ___ ing
by establishing
by founding
by inventing
by negotiating

PRACTICE EXERCISE

Complete each sentence with a "by _____ ing" expression.

Example:

He helped to spread learning *by establishing a public library.*

1. They earned their tuition by _____.

2. He passed his exam by _____.

3. Jim developed his muscles by _____.

4. Jane gained weight by _____.

5. The team won the championship by _____.

D. SPELLING

The sound [ər] is easy to recognize in its regular form, **-er**. For example:

her	print**er**
serve	teach**er**
certain	eag**er**
nervous	

Less common spellings for the sound [ər] are given below. Note that before **r**, the vowel [ə] has several different spellings.

-ear-	-or-	-ir-	-ur-
learn	word	fir (tree)	fur
earn	world	first	burn
heard	work	bird	hurt
pearl	doctor	sir	turn
earnest	worse	stir	urge
early		dirt	purse
		firm	curve
		girl	curtain
			curl

E. PARAPHRASE

FORMAL	COLLOQUIAL
1. He contributed greatly to his city.	1. He did a lot for his city.
2. He made many practical inventions.	2. He thought up lots of useful things.
3. earned Franklin world fame	3. made him famous all over
4. dedicated the last years of his life	4. gave his last years

F. IDIOMS

to this day = up to now
played a part = participated
drawing up a document = drafting an official paper
make a living = earn money to support oneself

G. SEMANTICS

These words are closely related in meaning:

practical = workable
efficient = giving good results, functioning well
useful = serving a purpose, good for something

PRACTICE EXERCISE

Use the correct word to complete each sentence (practical, efficient, useful).

1. This engine is very _____; it works well without wasting fuel.

2. When we plan a project, he often offers _____ suggestions.

3. A saw is a _____ tool for wood-working.

4. A fireplace is not as _____ as a modern heater.

H. COMPREHENSION

1. How did Franklin make a living when he was young?
2. What did he do for Philadelphia?
3. What made Franklin famous?
4. Why did he go to France?
5. What did Franklin do in his old age?

I. SPEAKING AND WRITING

Discussion

1. Do you think it was easier for a person to be an expert in many different things in those days than it is today?
2. Does your city need a person like Franklin? Why?
3. Can you imagine how Franklin traveled to France? How long and how comfortable would such a trip have been?
4. How do you think a person should spend his retirement years? Do you think Franklin had the right idea?

Summary

In a sentence or two tell what you learned about Franklin.

6

Thomas Jefferson, Man of Many Talents

Thomas Jefferson with the original Declaration of Independence. (The Old Print Shop)

architect

clever

originate

device

revolve

plow

achievement

declare

secure (*verb*)

consent

govern

inspire

brilliant

service

administer

Many of the leaders who helped to found the United States were highly cultured; yet even among them Thomas Jefferson stood out for his learning and his talents. He was a classical scholar, learned in Greek philosophy and in ancient literature. He was a successful lawyer. A gifted architect, he designed his beautiful home, Monticello (which still stands, near Charlottesville, Virginia), as well as the buildings of the University of Virginia. He was also a musician and a clever inventor, who originated many useful devices, including folding doors, revolving chairs, and an improved plow.

Jefferson's most outstanding achievement was as chief author of the Declaration of Independence, a great statement of human rights and liberties. It declares that all are created equal; that the purpose of government is "to secure the rights" of the people "to life, liberty, and the pursuit of happiness"; and that a government has power only "by the consent of the governed." This document has inspired people who believe in freedom all over the world and all through the years.

Jefferson also drew up the constitution for his state, Virginia, and served as its governor. He was sent to France as the foreign minister of the United States, and afterward was President Washington's Secretary of State. A few years later he became the country's third president, serving in that position for two terms.

After forty years of brilliant public service Jefferson left political life. In his remaining years he founded the University of Virginia, and acted as its administrator. This he considered his most important work, above all his political achievements.

A. PRONUNCIATION

"Long **o**" is pronounced with a [w] glide.

home [howm]

most [mowst]

only [own'li]

wrote [rowt]

go [gow]
no, know [now]
snow [snow]

B. WORD FORMATION

The ending **-ful** (meaning 'having' or 'characterized by') is added to nouns to form adjectives (see chapter 2, section B).

NOUN	ADJECTIVE
beauty	beautiful
success	successful
use	useful
joy	joyful
wonder	wonderful

PRACTICE EXERCISE

Use each of these adjectives with an appropriate noun.

Example:

a beautiful view

C. GRAMMAR

The relative pronoun **who** refers to the noun preceding it and is part of the clause that it begins. In the following examples, **who** is the subject of the verb that follows it. (In these sentences the subject of the relative clause is underlined with a single line, and the verb is underlined with a double line.)

a clever inventor (who originated many devices)

people (who believe in freedom)

the architect (who designed Monticello)

a scholar (who studied philosophy)

the minister (who was sent to France)

PRACTICE EXERCISE

Combine each pair of short sentences by changing the second sentence into a **who**-clause.

> Example:
>
> Jefferson was a political leader. Jefferson became President.
> Jefferson was a political leader who became President.

1. I met the author. He wrote the textbook.
2. She gave the book to a boy. The boy was going to the library.
3. We are students. We are learning English.
4. Jane is a singer. She hopes to become an opera star.
5. They spoke with the instructor. The instructor will teach the morning class.

D. SPELLING

The letters **-ign** are pronounced [ayn] like *mine, fine*.

> s**ign**
> al**ign**
> des**ign**
> res**ign**
> ass**ign**

E. PARAPHRASE

FORMAL	COLLOQUIAL
1. who originated devices	1. who thought up gadgets
2. by the consent of the governed	2. as long as the people agree
3. serving in the position	3. holding the job

F. IDIOMS

> stood out = was unusual
> all through the years = at all times, past and present
> all over; all over the world = everywhere

above all his political achievements = more important than all he had
done in politics

spent his last years ____ ing = devoted time and attention during his last
years

G. SEMANTICS

Note the distinction between the following words:

say = express in words

tell = give information or instructions

announce = make known publicly

declare = make known clearly or emphatically

proclaim = announce in an official manner

H. COMPREHENSION

1. What were Jefferson's special abilities?
2. What important documents did he write?
3. What were the highlights of his political career?
4. What did he do in his last years?

I. SPEAKING AND WRITING

Discussion

1. Jefferson has been referred to as a Renaissance man. Do you consider that a fitting term for him?
2. If a government may rule only "by consent of the governed," then who is the boss? Do you approve of such a government?
3. Why do you suppose Jefferson considered his involvement with the University of Virginia his most important work?

Summary

Briefly summarize what you learned about Jefferson.

7

The Yankee Clippers

A clipper ship, famous for speed and for beauty, which sailed around the world carrying exports and imports.

vessel	complete (*verb*)
merchant	renowned
tip (*noun*)	efficient
luxury	gold rush
product	supersede

From the nation's early days, American sailing vessels were used in trade with the Far East. Starting out from ports along the New England coast, these merchant ships made their way around the tip of South America and up the Pacific coast. They stopped at the Pacific Northwest to buy furs, which were exchanged in the Far East many months later for tea, spices, and Oriental luxury goods. These products were brought back to the United States when the round-the-world voyage was completed.

In the middle years of the nineteenth century these voyages were made in the world-renowned Yankee clipper ships, famous for their beauty. In fact, the clipper ships were so well-designed that they were the fastest wind-driven ships ever built. During the California gold rush, these efficient ships were much in demand because they made the trip from New York around Cape Horn to California in a record eighty days. By 1860, however, the steamship had begun to supersede the sailing vessel, and the day of the Yankee clipper's glory came to an end.

A. PRONUNCIATION

[I]	*versus*	[iy] (with the [y] glide)
this		these
ship		sheep
lip		leap
sit		seat
fit		feet
hill		heel
clipper		east
trip		tea
in		see
built		we
which		me

B. WORD FORMATION

A special group of prepositions beginning with the prefix **a-** are stressed on the second syllable. Here are some of them.

> around
> about
> along
> above
> against
> among

C. GRAMMAR

Prepositional phrases begin with a preposition and end with a noun or pronoun. They don't contain a verb.

> from the nation's early days
> with the Far East
> along the tip of South America
> up the Pacific coast
> at the Pacific Northwest
> for tea, spices, and luxury goods
> to the United States
> for their beauty
> during the gold rush
> from New York
> in eighty days

PRACTICE EXERCISE

Make up sentences using the prepositions around, about, along, above, against, and among. (See the description of prepositional phrases above).

Example:

He looked carefully *among all the papers.*

D. SPELLING

Before the endings -**er**, -**ed**, or -**ing**, a final single consonant following a single vowel is doubled. Doubling keeps the first vowel "short."

SINGLE	DOUBLE
clip	clipper
ship	shipping
stop	stopped
sit	sitting
step	stepped
hit	hitting
stir	stirring
occur	occurred
can	canning
bat	batter

PRACTICE EXERCISE

Write the -**ing** and -**ed** forms of the words listed below.

Example:

	-**ing**	-**ed**
park	parking	parked
refer	referring	referred

1. mail	5. stamp	9. hop	13. slam
2. pat	6. clap	10. grasp	14. found
3. start	7. call	11. wrap	15. pull
4. kill	8. rain	12. explain	16. defeat

E. PARAPHRASE

FORMAL	COLLOQUIAL
1. These efficient ships were much in demand.	1. Everybody wanted these good ships.
2. The day of the Yankee clipper's glory came to an end.	2. The clipper was through.

F. IDIOMS

made their way = traveled
came to an end = was finished
were in demand = were desired
in record time = faster than ever before

G. SEMANTICS

Far East—location
Oriental = having the character or fashion of the Far East

H. COMPREHENSION

1. Where did the clippers begin their voyage?
2. What did they bring back?
3. Why were the clippers famous?
4. Why were they no longer used?

I. SPEAKING AND WRITING

Discussion

1. Would you have liked being a sailor on a clipper ship? Why?
2. What kinds of climate would the crew of a clipper ship experience on the way from New England to the Pacific Northwest?
3. Are you sorry that this kind of ship is no longer used? Why?

Summary

Briefly tell what you learned about the Yankee clippers.

8

The Pueblo Indians

Taos Pueblo—an old group dwelling which is still lived in. (Denver Public Library)

impressive

structure

palace

hollowed

descendant

organized

craft

pottery

geometric

pattern

research

archaeology

glimpse

In Colorado's Mesa Verde National Park there is an impressive structure called the Cliff Palace. This huge building, dating back almost a thousand years, is partially hollowed out of the cliff and structured of adobe, a sun-baked clay. It once contained 200 rooms and was a kind of apartment house for a whole village of Indians. Descendants of those people, the Pueblo Indians of the southwestern 5 United States, still live in adobe houses of many rooms, sometimes large enough for the population of a village. Each Pueblo community closely organizes its political and social life and also maintains the old religious ceremonies.

The Pueblo Indians are farmers, but they also engage in fine craftwork. Their pottery is made by the women only. It is formed entirely by hand from long 10 coils of clay, and is decorated with geometric patterns. It is similar to the pottery of the Pueblos' ancestors of the twelfth and thirteenth centuries. The Pueblo Indians also do basketry and weaving. In recent years they have begun to make fine silver jewelry, often set with turquoise stones.

From accounts of sixteenth-century Spanish explorers and from the 15 research of archaeologists, we know that the ways of the Pueblos have not changed much from the ways of their ancestors. Their villages, such as the one in Taos, New Mexico, and others in the Southwest, give us a glimpse of one style of life of the American Indian past.

A. PRONUNCIATION

The verb ending **-ed** is not a separate syllable, unless its comes after the sound [t] or [d] (see chapter 2, section A).

called [kɔld]

hollowed [hal' owd]

contained [kən teynd']

baked [beykt]

organized [ɔr' gən ayzd]

formed [fɔrmd]

changed [čeynjd]

However, as we saw in chapter 2, section A(1), the **e** of the **-ed** verb ending *is* pronounced when preceded by [d] or [t].

constructed
loaded

B. WORD FORMATION

The adjective ending **-al** is pronounced [əl].

political	partial
social	formal
musical	vocal
final	typical

C. GRAMMAR

There beginning a clause or sentence with a **be** verb is an ''empty'' word without any meaning of its own. The subject comes after the **be** verb. When used this way, **there** is unstressed.

There is an impressive structure in the park.
There are many people in the room.
There was an accident on the highway.
There were two children there.
　(Is the last word an empty **there**?)

PRACTICE EXERCISE

Make up five sentences that describe your classroom, beginning each with **there** and a **be** verb. (Remember to use the singular or plural form of **be** to match the subject following it.) Underline the subject with a single line, and the verb with a double line.

Examples:

There are thirty chairs in the room.
There is a large desk for the teacher.

D. SPELLING

The sound [aw] as in *mouth* is usually spelled **ou** within a word; less often, **ow**.

thousand	found	towel
house	mouse	growl
south	about	down
sound	pound	crowd
count	around	frown

E. PARAPHRASE

FORMAL	COLLOQUIAL
1. There is an impressive structure.	1. There's a $\begin{cases} \text{big} \\ \text{grand} \end{cases}$ building.
2. constructed of adobe	2. made of clay
3. have not changed from the ways of their ancestors	3. kept the old life style
4. a glimpse of the American Indian past	4. a peek at the old life of the American Indians

F. IDIOMS

date back = happened at a past time
give us a glimpse = show us
such as = like, similar to

G. SEMANTICS

Words related in meaning:

An **archaeologist** studies ancient and prehistoric life.
An **explorer** investigates unknown regions.
A **discoverer** finds, or finds out, something not known before.

H. COMPREHENSION

1. What is the Cliff Palace?
2. What kind of villages do the Pueblo Indians have?

3. What kinds of craftwork do they produce?
4. How do they use turquoise?
5. What can we learn from the Pueblo villages?

I. SPEAKING AND WRITING

Discussion

1. Why do you suppose these buildings of adobe last long?
2. What kind of craftwork are you familiar with? Have you ever done such work?
3. Would you like to live as closely with your people as the Pueblo Indians do? Why?
4. Why do many people today live in large apartment houses? Why do you suppose the ancient Pueblos did so?

Summary

Briefly summarize the reading selection.

9

Architecture
of the Past

Independence Hall, Philadelphia, a Georgian-style building. (Philadelphia Redevelopment Authority)

imitation	adopt
environment	reconstruct
construction	stimulate
clapboard	dome
overlap	courtyard
cluster	lacy
comfortable	mission

American architecture began as imitation of what the early settlers were familiar with in their home countries, but it soon developed some special characteristics suited to the new environment. The New England colonists found that a new construction technique was needed in order to keep out the cold winter winds. With wood plentiful, they built clapboard houses by nailing horizontal boards so that the bottom edge of one board overlapped the upper edge of the board below it. Windows were kept small for warmth, and the heart of the house was a wide, high fireplace used for cooking as well as for heat. The white-painted clapboard house is still typical in New England. The houses of the early settlers were placed close together for safety, the usual plan being to cluster them around the central village green, with the church, the courthouse, and other public buildings on the same square. This arrangement can still be seen at the center of many New England towns.

In the frontier regions, of course, the log cabin was the standard type of house.

As conditions arose which called for larger buildings and more comfortable houses, the English Georgian style was widely adopted, with brick as the building material. Variations of the Georgian style are to be found all along the Eastern seaboard, particularly in the reconstructed Colonial town of Williamsburg, Virginia, and in Independence Hall and other eighteenth-century buildings in Philadelphia.

Great admiration for Greece, especially after the Greek wars of independence, stimulated classical (ancient Greek and Roman style) architecture. Classical buildings are symmetrical, dignified stone structures with a row of pillars at the front, and sometimes a dome. This style was used in the older government buildings of Washington, D.C., and in some of the state capitals. It was also adopted for mansions of plantation owners, some of which are still standing in the Carolinas, Louisiana, Mississippi, and other parts of the Old South.

A very different kind of architecture is to be seen in the old quarter of New Orleans, with houses built around hidden arcaded courtyards. The fronts facing the street are ringed with rows of lacy ironwork balconies.

From the Pacific coast to San Antonio, Texas, there are examples of mission style buildings constructed by Spanish colonists in the late eighteenth century. Spanish baroque architecture was the model for these buildings, which are usually of white or light-colored adobe with red tile roofs. Most impressive is the string of missions along the 600 miles of El Camino Real from San Diego, California, to Sonoma.

All these historic styles have been imitated in some modern buildings and houses.

35

A. PRONUNCIATION

Vowels with weakest stress are often pronounced [ə] in English.

> condition [kən dI′ šən]
> suitable [suwt′ ə bəl]
> environment [ɛn vay′ rən mənt]
> construction [kən strʌk′ šən]

When the place of stress changes, the sound of the vowel may change accordingly.

atom [æ′ təm]	atomic [ə tam′ Ik]
console [kən sowl′]	consolation [kan sə ley′ šən]
combine [kəm bayn′]	combination [kam bə ney′ šən]
family [fæm′ ə li]	familiar [fə mIl′ yər]

B. WORD FORMATION

Noun endings **-tion** and **-sion** (both pronounced like *shun*, but without stress):

imitation	mansion
construction	mission
condition	tension
admiration	pension

C. GRAMMAR

The infinitive can be used to express purpose in three ways: by itself (**to** _____), or with the expressions **in order to** or **so as to**.

Examples:
They built clapboard houses

> *to keep out* the winter winds.
> *in order to keep out* the winter winds.
> *so as to keep out* the winter winds.

They had awnings over the windows

> *to shade* them from the sun.
> *in order to shade* them from the sun.
> *so as to shade* them from the sun.

The people of old New Orleans had their houses built around enclosed courtyards

> *to have* privacy in their gardens.
> *in order to have* privacy.
> *so as to have* privacy.

PRACTICE EXERCISE

Answer the following questions, using each of these three ways of expressing purpose.

> Example:
>
> Why is he working after school?
> *to earn* some money for his expenses.
> *in order to earn* some money.
> *so as to earn* some money.

1. Why is Tom studying so hard?
2. Why are you planting these seeds?
3. Why are you saving the money?
4. Why do they jog every day?
5. Why did you go to the library?

D. SPELLING

The letter **a** in a closed syllable (that is, before a final consonant or before two or more consonants) represents the vowel [æ].

began	example	bat—batting
grass	fact	can—canned

overlap	demand	man—manning
classic	map	sad—sadder
mansion	bad	nap—napping
had	fact	slam—slamming

E. PARAPHRASE

FORMAL	COLLOQUIAL
1. began as an imitation of the buildings	1. started off by copying the buildings
2. a new construction technique	2. a new way of building
3. Another kind is to be seen in New Orleans.	3. In New Orleans you can see another kind.

F. IDIOMS

were familiar with = knew about

was widely adopted = was accepted by many people

The building is still standing. = The building still $\begin{cases} \text{exists.} \\ \text{remains.} \end{cases}$

G. SEMANTICS

Don't confuse **adopt** and **adapt**.

adopt = (1) take or accept by choice; (2) take up and use regularly

Because they admired the Greeks, they adopted the classical style.

The couple adopted an orphan.

They adopted this as their regular practice.

adapt = alter something to make it suitable or fit for a purpose.

They adapted the style to the modern urban situation.

The motor was adapted for use in a sawmill.

H. COMPREHENSION

1. Why did the settlers have to make changes in their method of building?
2. In what style were many of the older government buildings constructed?
3. Where would you go to see examples of the Georgian style?
4. What is the special characteristic of the old New Orleans buildings?

5. Who built the old missions? Where?

I. SPEAKING AND WRITING

Discussion

1. Are you familiar with towns built around a central square or place? Where?
2. Why do you suppose old New Orleans reminds some people of Spain?
3. Do you know for what purpose the old missions were built?
4. If you wanted to take a trip to see American historical architecture, how would you plan it?

Summary

Briefly summarize what you learned in this selection.

10

Utopian Settlements

"Tree of Light" by Hannah Cahoon, 1845, an example of Shaker craftsmanship. (Hancock Shaker Village Library)

Utopia	discrimination
idealistic	sect
ideology	ecstasy
commune	abolish
celibate	recent
segregated	alienation

In its earlier years, the United States seemed to many groups of people to be a good place for idealistic experiments in living. A number of settlements were established here on the basis of particular ideologies, largely religious or socialistic.

Among the most interesting of the religious colonies were those of the Shakers. They were followers of Ann Lee, an English woman who claimed to be a female Christ reborn. In 1774, after they had suffered persecution and imprisonment in England, the Shakers came to the United States to found their first commune.

In the Shaker communes all members were celibate. Men and women were segregated, but the women had as much power and respect in the community as the men, and there was no racial discrimination. It was a very strict religious sect, with members dancing in esctasy at their religious ceremonies. (In fact, people began to call them "Shakers" because of their excited dancing, and finally that became their name.) They made beautiful handicrafts and furniture, which are highly prized to this day.

At their height the Shakers had eighteen vigorous and successful comunes in various parts of the country. Today only a handful of members remain, loyally praying and working according to the rules of their sect.

In the early 1800s the famous British industrialist Robert Owen, who devoted himself to helping factory workers, bought a place in Indiana for a cooperative colony. In this settlement, called New Harmony, each family got food and goods from a public store. Instead of money they used credits earned by working. Although New Harmony did not last long, it initiated many excellent projects, which have been imitated by others. The group established a free school and a free library; they also worked to abolish imprisonment for debt, and they helped newly-freed slaves.

Many other leaders and sects have founded Utopian communities in accordance with their beliefs. During the late 1960s some communes were founded by opponents of U.S. involvement in Vietnam. In recent years a number of cooperative communes have been established by people trying to escape the competitiveness and alienation of modern society.

A. PRONUNCIATION

The "long **a**" [ey] is a diphthong, pronounced with a glide.

place	sail
basis	came
Shakers	States
claim	they
female	day
	way

Can you hear and pronounce the difference between the following pairs of words?

[ey]	*versus*	[ɛ]
tale		tell
jail		jell
fail		fell
sail		sell
gate		get
late		let
mate		met
wait		wet
main		men
pain		pen
trade		tread
raid		red
lace		less

B. WORD FORMATION

	ADJECTIVE	NOUN
	high	height
but		
	wide	width
	long	length
	deep	depth

Practice pronouncing *width*, *length*, *depth*, so that both final consonant sounds are clear.

C. GRAMMAR

1. Past perfect tense (which uses **had** as auxiliary) refers to past action that is more remote than another past event or time.
> a. After they had suffered persecution, they came here.
>> (First they suffered persecution; then they came here.)
> b. I had waited for an hour before he arrived.
>> (First I waited for an hour; then he arrived.)
> c. By noon yesterday, he had read the whole book.
>> (Noon was past; the reading was before that.)
> d. They ate the food which she had prepared.
>> (First she prepared the food; then they ate it.)

PRACTICE EXERCISE

Complete these sentences, being careful to use the correct tense of the verb that you choose.

Example:

After he had finished the job, he *went* out.

1. We had rung the bell four times; finally ⎯⎯⎯⎯⎯⎯⎯⎯⎯⎯.
2. It had snowed all night, but ⎯⎯⎯⎯⎯⎯⎯⎯⎯⎯.
3. Although I had met him before, ⎯⎯⎯⎯⎯⎯⎯⎯⎯⎯.
4. Suddenly she ⎯⎯⎯⎯⎯⎯⎯⎯ where she had left it.
5. After he had paid his bill, ⎯⎯⎯⎯⎯⎯⎯⎯⎯⎯.

2. The verb **do** (past tense **did**) is used as an auxiliary in questions. When a statement with a one-word verb (other than *be*) is changed to a question, the auxiliary **do** (present) or **did** (past) comes before the subject. In a short answer to such a question, **do** or **did** can be used instead of the whole verb, or instead of the verb and what follows it.
> a. Do the members share the work? (a question based on the statement ''The members share the work.'')
>> Yes, they do.
>> Yes, they share the work.
> b. Did Owen found New Harmony? (based on ''Owen founded New Harmony.'')
>> Yes, he did.
>> Yes, he founded it.

    c. Did the colony last long?
        No, it didn't.
        No, it didn't last long.
    d. Do you like school?
        Yes, I do.
        Yes, I like it very much.

PRACTICE EXERCISE

Give both short and long answers to these questions. (Remember to use **does—not**, **do**—in the present with a third person singular subject).

    Examples:

    Did you write the composition?
        Yes, I did.
        Yes, I wrote it.
    Does Jack have a job?
        No, he doesn't.
        No, he doesn't have a job.

1. Does Eleanor play tennis?
2. Did you find your keys?
3. Does the bus stop at this corner?
4. Do your parents live in New York?
5. Does your class meet at ten o'clock?
6. Do the students use the language lab?
7. Did Jane go to the party?

D. SPELLING

A regular or common spelling for the sound [ey] is **-ai-**. At the end of a word it is **-ay**.

ai		ay
claim	main	pay
remain	chair	say
train	sail	play
rain	aim	day
maid	aid	may

There are special spellings for the sound [ey] in some words, for example:

they	**eigh**t
their	w**eigh**
there	n**eigh**bor

E. PARAPHRASE

FORMAL	COLLOQUIAL
1. The women had power.	1. The women had clout.
2. They experimented in ways of living.	2. They tried out new life styles.
3. They were in ecstasy.	3. They were carried away.
4. Only a few remain.	4. There are just a few left.

F. IDIOMS

on the basis of = following the ideas or principles of
in accordance with = conforming to; in harmony with
at its height = when it was most successful
set up = establish

G. SEMANTICS

Some confusing pairs of words:
find (*past tense:* found) = discover; locate
found (*past tense:* founded) = establish
  She always finds time to read. He found what he was looking for.
  Owen founded a Utopian colony.

price = cost
prize = reward; winning
  What is the price of this book?
  He hopes to win the prize.

religion = belief
sect = a group (usually small) with a common religious belief
  Buddhism is an Eastern religion.
  The Society of Friends is a sect also known as the Quakers.

H. COMPREHENSION

1. What did the Shakers produce?
2. What good ideas did the New Harmony colony introduce?
3. What kind of economy did New Harmony have? How did its members buy and trade?

I. SPEAKING AND WRITING

Discussion

1. Why do you suppose people establish Utopian colonies?
2. Would you like to live in a Utopian colony? If so, a colony based on what idea?
3. Did some immigrants look on the United States itself as a Utopia?
4. Why did most of the Utopian colonies finally change or break up?

Summary

Summarize this selection in two or three sentences.

11

The Underground Railroad and Harriet Tubman

The Underground Railroad—members helping an escaped slave to a "station" and to freedom.

decade	ingenious
founder (*noun*)	disguise
risk	dangerous
fine (*noun*)	rescue
territory	extraordinary
singly	ingenuity
transportation	

For several decades before the Civil War, which brought an end to slavery, a secret operation was carried on for the purpose of freeing slaves. This was known as the Underground Railroad. Its founders were the Abolitionists, people active in the movement to abolish slavery in the United States. Many Northern whites worked in the Underground Railroad, as well as some blacks; even a number of Southern whites, including former slaveholders, took part in it. Risking fines, imprisonment, and even death, some of these people went into the slave states, picked up slaves who had run away or who wished to do so, and led them northward into free territory. Singly or in small groups, the escaping slaves would be brought to a "station." This was, as a rule, the home of a member of the "organization," who would hide them and take care of them until a wagon or other means of transportation could take them (usually at night) to another station farther north. In this way, many escaping slaves finally reached Canada and sure freedom. So long as they were within the United States, they were in danger of being found and claimed by their owners.

Many ingenious disguises and tricks were used in covering up this dangerous activity. It is estimated that 75,000 slaves were freed through the Underground Railroad.

A remarkable leader in this operation was Harriet Tubman, herself a runaway slave. She had the courage to return secretly to the South nineteen times, rescuing more than three hundred slaves. She knew many back roads and secret paths, and knew what drugs could be given to children to keep them from crying. She had unusual strength and displayed extraordinary bravery and ingenuity. She was indeed a great American heroine.

A. PRONUNCIATION

w as a shortened [u] sound:

war	**well**	**wagon**
which	**within**	**wish**

was	white	runaway
work	would	

B. WORD FORMATION

The suffix **-er** added to a verb makes a noun that means 'one who does something'.

found—founder	write—writer
teach—teacher	sing—singer
work—worker	swim—swimmer
lead—leader	play—player
own—owner	

PRACTICE EXERCISE

Replace the **-er** noun in each sentence with the matching verb.

Examples:

Tom is a good singer.
   Tom sings well.
Franklin was the founder of the college.
   Franklin founded the college.

1. Smith is a hockey player.
2. They are good dancers.
3. Mr. and Mrs. Jones were the owners of this house.
4. Jane is a reader of novels.
5. The members were followers of Robert Owen.
6. She was a singer in the choir.
7. The men are workers in the factory.
8. Both of his parents are teachers.

C. GRAMMAR

For correct use of the article in English, it is important to know whether a noun is a count nount. A count noun refers to items that can be counted; it may be used in the singular or in the plural. Noncount nouns include mass nouns like *air, water, coal, gold, sand, coffee, rice, butter, tennis, music,* and *information,* and generalizations (ideas) like *truth, courage, love, democracy,* and *slavery.* Such nouns are never plural. A singular count noun *must* have an article (**a** or **the**), or another determiner (**this, that, one, each, every**), or a possessive. A noncount noun never has the indefinite article (**a**); it may or may not have the definite article (**the**). (The use of the definite article with noncount nouns is explained in chapter 42, section C 2.)

> Examples of singular count nouns, with articles:
> *The man* was *an Abolitionist.*
> *A slave* was brought to *a station.*
> *The slaveholder* tried to get *the slave* back.
> During *the night, a wagon* stopped at *the house* to take *that slave* to *the* next *station,* which was *the home* of *a member* of *the organization.*

> Examples of noncount nouns (no article, no plural):
> They were against *slavery.*
> He believes in *peace* and *brotherhood.*
> Harriet Tubman had *courage* and *strength.*
> Franklin experimented with *electricity.*
> She drinks *coffee* without *cream* or *sugar.*
> I am studying *art, mathematics,* and *chemistry.*

PRACTICE EXERCISE

Fill in each blank that requires an article or other determiner before the following noun.

> Examples:
>
> They heat *the* house with _____ oil.
> I bought *a* book about _____ chemistry.

1. We believe in _____ democracy.

2. She went to _____ store to buy _____ coffee.

3. _____ tire needs _____ air.

4. _____ ring is made of _____ gold.

5. He never buys _____ books; he just borrows them from _____ library.

6. _____ boy studies _____ music.

7. _____ girl is studying to be _____ teacher.

8. _____ doctor gave _____ man _____ prescription.

D. SPELLING

Study the following irregular spellings:

would [wʊd]	brought [brɔt]
should [šʊd]	death [dɛθ]
could [kʊd]	southern [sʌð′ ərn]
night [nayt]	courage [kʌr′ Ij]
disguise [dIs gayz′]	ingenious [In jiyn′ yəs]

E. PARAPHRASE

FORMAL	COLLOQUIAL
1. A secret operation was carried on for the purpose of freeing slaves.	1. They had an undercover setup for freeing slaves.
2. She displayed extraordinary bravery.	2. She had guts.
3. They were taken to a secret station.	3. They were sneaked off to a hideout.

F. IDIOMS

pick up = take
so long as = while
covering up = hiding
keep them from = prevent them from
take part = participate

G. SEMANTICS

prevent = not let something happen
  Being careful can prevent some accidents.

abolish = make something stop; put an end to something
  They hope to abolish war.

H. COMPREHENSION

1. Who took part in the Underground Railroad?
2. Was it dangerous? How?
3. What happened at a "station"?
4. Why do we call Harriet Tubman a heroine?

I. SPEAKING AND WRITING

Discussion

1. Do you suppose all slaves wished to escape? Why?
2. Were the Abolitionists right in conducting their illegal activity?
3. What would most people expect a person like Harriet Tubman to do after she first escaped?
4. Why do you suppose whites, including some Southerners, worked in the Underground Railroad organization?

Summary

Explain the Underground Railroad and what it accomplished.

12

The Old-Time Farmer

Old-time farming—cultivating the soil with a horse-drawn plow. (U.S. Department of Agriculture)

independent	olden days	spade	transact
self-sufficient	dawn	scythe	gossip
surplus	chore	pitchfork	elementary
rural	ax	recreation	self-reliant

Traditionally, the American farmer has always been independent and hard-working. In the eighteenth century farmers were quite self-sufficient. The farm family grew and made almost everything it needed. The surplus crop would be sold to buy a few items in the local general store.

In 1860, although some of the farm population had moved to the city, eighty percent of the American population was still rural. In the late nineteenth century, farm work and life were not much changed from what they had been in olden days. Farmers arose at dawn or before and had many chores to do, with their muscles as their chief source of power. They used axes, spades, scythes, pitchforks, and other simple tools. Cooking was done in wood-burning stoves, and the kerosene lamp was the only improvement on the candle. The family's recreation and social life consisted chiefly of a drive in the wagon to the nearby small town or village to transact some business as well as to exchange gossip with neighbors who had also come to town.

The children attended a small elementary school (often of just one room) to which they had to walk every day, possibly for a few miles. The school term was short so that the children could help on the farm.

Although the whole family worked, and life was not easy, farmers as a class were self-reliant and independent.

A. PRONUNCIATION

[č] can be pronounced [tš]; [j] can be pronounced [dž].

[č] (voiceless)	*versus*	[j] (voiced)
chore		**g**eneral
chiefly		**j**ust
children		lar**g**ely
ea**ch**		e**dg**e
chur**ch**		**j**u**dg**e
chin		en**g**ine
cheap		**j**eep
choke		**j**oke
cheer		**j**eer
chair		**j**ar
	chan**g**e	

B. WORD FORMATION

Noun compounds are formed by attaching two words, the first of which receives heavier stress.

pitchfork	**bed**room	**court**yard
schoolhouse	**check**book	**book**case

Many noun compounds are written as two words; a few are written with a hyphen. Regardless of spelling (as one word, two words, or hyphenated), the compound is always stressed on its *first* part.

lighthouse	**card** table	**sun**-shower
earthquake	**play** room	**great**-aunt
lifeboat	**farm** work	**fighter**-bomber

The stress pattern of noun compounds is important because in some combinations the meaning is different when the same words are used separately (not as a compound). In that case the *second* word is stressed. Notice the difference between the following:

COMPOUND	NOT COMPOUND

the **White** House
    (residence of the President)
	a white **house**
	    (a house that is white)

moving van
    (a truck for hauling)
	moving **van**
	    (a van that is in motion)

Spanish teacher
    (one who teaches Spanish)
	Spanish **teacher**
	    (a teacher from Spain)

blackbird
    (a species of bird)
	black **bird**
	    (a bird of black color)

greenhouse
    (a place for growing plants)
	green **house**
	    (a house painted green)

PRACTICE EXERCISE

1. Guess the meaning of the following noun compounds. (Note that in noun compounds the second word tells what the thing is and the first word classifies, or describes, it.)

Examples:

songbird—a *bird* that sings
birdcage—a *cage* for a bird
orange juice—*juice* from oranges

1. homeland
2. notebook
3. swimsuit
4. roadmap
5. wristwatch
6. birthday
7. tablecloth
8. wallpaper
9. bus tour
10. bookstore
11. doghouse
12. classroom

2. Make up a compound word for each of the meanings listed.

   Examples:

   shoes for walking in deep snow—snowshoes
   a brush for spreading paint—paintbrush

   1. a mine for (digging out) coal
   2. a room for dining ('eating')
   3. a lamp that lights by burning oil
   4. a box for carrying lunch
   5. skates that are used on ice
   6. a cup for tea
   7. a knife for spreading butter
   8. a hat to protect (the head) from rain

C. GRAMMAR

-ing words made from verbs can be used as nouns. When used this way they are called *gerunds*.

   Cooking was done on stoves.
   They enjoy cooking.
   Swimming is good exercise.
   He developed his muscles by swimming.
   He found it by looking in the closet.
   Studying requires patience.
   Guessing is quite different from knowing.

D. SPELLING

The sound [j] is spelled **j**, or **g** (before **i**, **e**, or **y**), or sometimes **dg**.

jet	age	edge
major	page	smudge
just	gentle	budge
joy	gym	budget
jump	agent	judge
object	region	trudge
injection	ginger	badge
join	wages	wedge

Note: The **di** in *soldier* is pronounced [j].

E. PARAPHRASE

FORMAL	COLLOQUIAL
1. He was independent and hardworking.	1. He was a go-getter.
2. to exchange gossip	2. to gab
3. the surplus	3. what was left over
4. recreation	4. fun; good time

F. IDIOMS

to do chores = to perform daily tasks around the house or farm
was his own man; was his own boss = was independent
stood on his own two feet = was self-reliant

G. SEMANTICS

Words of related meaning:

dawn = first appearance of daylight
daybreak = the very beginning of day
sunrise = time when the sun rises over the horizon

H. COMPREHENSION

1. What made the farm family self-sufficient?
2. How did they earn some money?
3. What kind of power was used on the farm?
4. What was the weekly "good time"?
5. What kind of school did the children attend?

I. SPEAKING AND WRITING

Discussion

1. Have you ever seen farm life like that?
2. Do you suppose the old-time farm family was happy? Why?
3. Were the farmer's tools and fuel very different from what they had been hundreds (or even thousands) of years before?
4. Would you have liked to grow up on a farm in those days?

Summary

Briefly tell how farmers lived in the 1800s.

13

Thoreau,
a Hundred Years Later

Walden, near the spot where Thoreau built his cabin.

naturalist	allow
individual	resist
impressed	convenience
servant	surroundings
interfere	frugal
accordance	inspiration
actually	appreciation

Henry David Thoreau was a writer and naturalist who lived in the nine-teenth century. He believed in living close to nature and in the freedom of the individual. Although he was impressed with the power and beauty of the new steam trains, he worried about the possible effects of rapid transportation on people's lives. He was also afraid that modern machines would become the ⁵ masters rather than the servants of people. In addition he opposed a strong government because it might interfere with people's freedom.

Thoreau tried to live in accordance with his ideas. As a protest against slavery, he actually went to prison rather than pay taxes to a government that allowed it. In his book *Civil Disobedience* he wrote about the principle of peace- ¹⁰ fully resisting what a person judges to be immoral acts of government. His most famous book, *Walden*, explains many of his ideas. It also tells about his daily life in a simple cabin that he himself had built near a pond in the woods. He had left the convenience and pleasures of his city home to live alone in natural surround-ings. There he lived frugally, providing most of his needs from what he found ¹⁵ around him.

For many years the ideas of Thoreau were known to scholars and to thinkers but not to the general public. However, in the middle years of this century he became the inspiration of many young people dissatisfied with the machine age and with modern ways of life. These people were impressed with his ²⁰ opposition to powerful government, and with his courage in living according to his beliefs. They also welcomed his appreciation of nature and of plain living. Thus Thoreau became the guide and ideal of many Americans a century and more after his death.

A. PRONUNCIATION

[č] is the pronunciation for **t** before a suffix beginning with the letter **u**.

nature [ney′ čər]	furniture [fər′ nə čər]
natural [næč′ ə rəl]	century [sɛn′ čə ri]
actually [æk′ ču ə li]	mixture [mIks′ čər]

B. WORD FORMATION

Some words ending in **f** (or **f** plus silent **e**) change the **f** to **v** before the plural ending.

SINGULAR	PLURAL
life	lives
knife	knives
wife	wives
leaf	leaves
half	halves
loaf	loaves
thief	thieves

PRACTICE EXERCISE

In a dictionary, look up the plural form of each of these nouns.

1. roof
2. scarf
3. safe
4. cuff
5. calf
6. belief

C. GRAMMAR

When a one-word verb (except **be**) becomes negative, **do** (**does**) is used as auxiliary in the present, and **did** in the past. The order of the words is: *subject, auxiliary* (**do, does,** or **did**), **not,** *verb.* The word **not** after the auxiliary is often shortened to **n't** and attached to the auxiliary. The shortened form is usually used in informal speaking, and the longer form is used in writing.

He lives in the country.

He $\begin{Bmatrix} \text{does not} \\ \text{doesn't} \end{Bmatrix}$ live there.

They oppose slavery.

They $\begin{Bmatrix} \text{do not} \\ \text{don't} \end{Bmatrix}$ oppose slavery.

Thoreau built his cabin himself.

He $\begin{Bmatrix} \text{did not} \\ \text{didn't} \end{Bmatrix}$ build the cabin.

Some people like Thoreau's ideas.

Others $\begin{Bmatrix} \text{do not} \\ \text{don't} \end{Bmatrix}$ like his ideas.

PRACTICE EXERCISE

Change the following sentences to the negative. (Remember that **be** verbs and verbs of more than one word don't use the **do** auxiliary with the negative.)

Examples:

She plays tennis.

She $\begin{Bmatrix} \text{doesn't} \\ \text{does not} \end{Bmatrix}$ play tennis.

Mr. Smith is a teacher.

Mr. Smith $\begin{Bmatrix} \text{isn't} \\ \text{is not} \end{Bmatrix}$ a teacher.

1. The man went to prison.
2. The book explains his ideas.
3. People were eager to see it.
4. He lived simply.
5. There are many books in this library.

D. SPELLING

Both **ou** and **ow** are spellings for the sound [aw].

surround	allow
about	plow
around	now
found	how
ground	cow
sound	power
loud	flower
boundary	shower
our	
hour	

In many words **ow** is the spelling for the sound [ow], especially at the end of a word.

show	low
blow	below
snow	flow
slow	grow

E. PARAPHRASE

FORMAL	COLLOQUIAL
1. interfere with his freedom	1. boss him around
2. disturbed about the possible effects	2. worried about what might come of it
3. machines would become the masters	3. machines would run people's lives
4. He lived frugally.	4. He got along with very little.
5. He was their inspiration.	5. They looked up to him.

F. IDIOMS

was impressed with = admired
making out = providing for himself
the general public = most people; people as a whole

G. SEMANTICS

civil disobedience = refusal to obey government rules as a matter of principle in the attempt to influence the government

peaceful resistance = showing objection to a policy of the government by not cooperating, but avoiding violence

simple living = living without luxury

a strong government = a government with great power

H. COMPREHENSION

1. What did Thoreau believe in?
2. What did he think about modern technology (new machinery)?

3. How did he feel that the individual should show his objections to his government's actions when they seemed to be wrong?
4. What does his book *Walden* tell?
5. What do young people today admire about Thoreau?

I. SPEAKING AND WRITING

Discussion

1. How can machines become the masters of people?
2. Is it easy to live as you believe? Is it worth the sacrifices?
3. Are there pleasures in simple living like Thoreau's life at Walden pond? What are they?
4. Which of Thoreau's ideas have special meaning today?

Summary

Briefly tell what you learned about Thoreau—in your own words.

14

Westward
to the Mississippi

Covered wagons—pioneers traveling in the wilderness. (Denver Public Library)

opportunity   hostile
penetrate   arched
legend   possessions
mountain pass   threat
migrant   enclosure
rutted   crude

Even before the United States became a nation, some of its people began
to move west. Many were attracted by the promise of new opportunities; some, by
the search for adventure. In fact, the westward movement has continued throughout the history of the United States.

  The first to penetrate the unknown lands west of the Appalachian Moun-   5
tains were the trappers and fur traders, whose trails were later followed by actual
settlers. There are many legends about Daniel Boone, a trapper and wilderness
expert, who led courageous people through a steep pass in the mountains.

  As the years passed, other pioneers went on to areas still farther west,
toward the Mississippi River. Some families moved more than once, looking for   10
better land. The migrants encountered many hardships—muddy, rutted trails, bad
weather, illness, hunger, and sometimes hostile Indians. Many died during the
journey and were buried along the way. Still the pioneers kept moving westward—on foot, on horseback, and in covered wagons. The arched cloth roofs of
these wagons gave some protection from the weather for the travelers and for their   15
few possessions. In fact, the covered wagons could even float across a stream.
When there was a threat of Indian attack, the wagons of a party would be arranged
in a circle. The women and children would hide within the enclosure, while the
men stood guard outside, prepared to fight if necessary.

  When they reached the place where they wished to settle, the pioneers   20
built log cabins. These crude shelters had no windows and no floors. Wooden
shelves along the wall were used as beds. A fireplace served both for warmth and
for cooking. The men would go off to hunt in the woods, while the women did all
the other work. Neighbors usually gathered to help each other in building a cabin
or a barn, and in other difficult tasks. To celebrate completion of the work, they   25
would all join in a merry party.

  After the settlers had cleared the land and started farming, living conditions slowly began to improve. More comfortable houses were built, and the
women tried to bring some beauty as well as convenience into the home.

A. PRONUNCIATION

Consonant groups: Pronounce such groups carefully, so that each consonant is heard.

threat	ar**ch**ed
through	comp**l**etion
har**dsh**ip	lege**nds**
roo**fs**	**impr**ove
horse**b**ack	**st**ates
chil**dr**en	**st**ill
arran**ged**	shel**ves**
war**mth**	wes**tw**ard

B. WORD FORMATION

1. The suffix **-ward** means 'in that direction' or 'toward'. It is pronounced like *word*, but without stress. (The word *toward* is an exception: it is pronounced [tɔrd].)

westward

onward

downward

homeward

outward

2. Some **-ant** nouns are based on **-ate** verbs.

VERB	NOUN (or ADJECTIVE)
migrate	migrant
immigrate	immigrant
emigrate	emigrant

The one who migrates is a migrant.
The one who immigrates is an immigrant.

PRACTICE EXERCISE

Fill in each blank, using *migrate*, *immigrate*, or *emigrate*, or one of the **-ant** nouns based on these verbs.

Examples:

Many Quakers *immigrated* to America.

1. These birds _____ southward every October; they are _____ birds.

2. Most of the people of the United States are _____ or the descendants of _____, who _____ from their homeland in search of a better life.

C. GRAMMAR

For "who" questions, the answer replaces **who** with a noun or pronoun, and replaces the verb (except the verb **be**) with **do** (present) or **did** (past).

    Who guided some early pioneers?
        Daniel Boone.
  or Daniel Boone did.
    Who hid in the enclosure?
        The women and children.
  or The women and children did.
    Who built the cabins?
        The pioneers.
  or The pioneers did.

PRACTICE EXERCISE

Answer these "who" questions, using both forms presented in the preceding examples.

1. Who drives the school bus?
2. Who lost this wallet?
3. Who wants to go with us?
4. Who borrowed my book?
5. Who knows the answer?

D. SPELLING

A common spelling for the sound [ey] is **a** + consonant(s) + **e**.

rate	same	penetrate
hate	came	later
date	fade	courageous
tale	place	celebrate
sale	take	relate
sane	mistake	arrange

E. PARAPHRASE

FORMAL	COLLOQUIAL
1. The movement continued.	1. The movement went on.
2. The fireplace served for warmth.	2. The fireplace was used to keep warm.
3. throughout its history	3. all through its history
4. encountered hardships	4. had a hard time had it tough

F. IDIOMS

$$\text{stand guard} = \text{be} \begin{cases} \text{on guard} \\ \text{watching} \end{cases} \text{in order to protect}$$

keep (on)* going = continue going
keep (on) working = continue working
keep (on) looking = continue looking

$$\text{They went} \begin{cases} \text{on foot.} \\ \text{on horseback.} \\ \text{by rail.} \\ \text{by ship.} \\ \text{by air (by airplane).} \end{cases}$$

G. SEMANTICS

Closely related words:

trail—very narrow, made by walking
a hiking trail

road—for wagons or cars
a muddy dirt road

highway—wide, paved
a six-lane highway

street—in the city
a business street

lane—in the country
a pleasant lane for walking

*On is usually used for action that continues steadily without stops.

seek—try to find
seek advice
search—look carefully, thoroughly
search the neighborhood, looking for the lost child

H. COMPREHENSION

1. Why did the people move west?
2. What did Daniel Boone do?
3. What troubles did the migrants have?
4. What was the covered wagon?
5. How was it used for protection?

I. SPEAKING AND WRITING

Discussion

1. Can you imagine the life of a woman on the journey westward, and her life in the wilderness?
2. Do you know of any community or folk celebration marking the completion of a hard job? Describe it.

Summary

In two or three sentences tell what you learned about this migration.

15

The California Gold Rush

Forty-niners in a gold-mining camp. (Denver Public Library)

remote	channel
undeveloped	determination
discover	fierce
prospector	competition
sieve	rough
search	uproot
precious	livelihood
speck	influx

In 1848 a settler in remote, undeveloped California discovered gold near Sacramento. As the news spread, a great tide of gold-hungry men flowed in to California. These "Forty-niners" (migrants of 1849) came from all parts of the United States in the tens of thousands. There were even gold-seekers from Europe. Some of the people moved across the country by wagon, traveling almost   5
half a year and meeting many hardships and dangers. Others sailed all the way around South America, finally reaching the California shore. Since the first discovery was of tiny pieces of gold at the bottom of a stream, many of the prospectors used pans and sieves, searching the waters of brooks and rivers for the precious specks of yellow metal. Others made channels to draw off flowing water   10
in order to examine it carefully for specks of gold. They worked with almost insane determination and fierce competition.

Life was rough in the days of the California gold rush. A few of the adventurers became rich, but most of them were bitterly disappointed. After uprooting themselves from home and from livelihood and after traveling the long,   15
dangerous road to California, they had found little or nothing. Some returned home. But many remained in California to work and to settle without the riches they had dreamed of possessing.

It was this great influx of people that built up California and led to its becoming a state of the United States in 1850.   20

A. PRONUNCIATION

At the beginning of a syllable **h** is pronounced as a puff of breath.

hungry	hole	inhale
hardship	hill	behave
hand	have	inhabit
half [hæf]	home	rehearse
hard	hot	adhesive
here	hat	
how	hair	

The **h** is not pronounced at all in *hour, honest, honor,* and words related to them (such as *hourly, honorable*), and in a few other words.

B. WORD FORMATION

Three confusingly similar verbs are **flow**, **fly**, and **flee**.

PRESENT (*base form*)	PAST (*one-word verb*)	PAST PARTICIPLE (*after* have, has, had)
flow	flowed	(have) flowed
fly	flew	(have) flown
flee	fled	(have) fled

flow = move like a liquid
      The stream flowed down to the valley.
fly = move through the air
      The plane flew above the clouds.
      The birds had already flown south.
flee = run away from danger or from trouble.
      They fled from the burning house.

PRACTICE EXERCISE

Fill in the blanks with the correct form of the verbs *flow*, *fly*, or *flee*.

1. The Pilgrims _____ from religious persecution.

2. The river _____ slowly on this hot, still summer day.

3. We looked up as the planes _____ above.

4. Have you ever _____ over the ocean?

5. The cat _____ from the barking dog.

6. When the child let the balloon go, it _____ right up.

C. GRAMMAR

More noncount nouns. These are mass nouns or generalizations (ideas) and are used without an article (see chapter 11, section C).

Gold attracts many people.
Life was rough in the mining camps.
They hoped to find *wealth*.
Water is a necessity of *life*.
Some people think only of *money*.

PRACTICE EXERCISE

Write an article in the blank if the noun that follows is a count noun; do not fill it in if that noun is a mass noun or a generalization.

1. _____ man said that _____ health is more important than _____ wealth.

2. They had a great deal of _____ trouble.

3. _____ doctor told _____ woman not to use _____ salt.

4. They suffer from _____ poverty and _____ ignorance, and they don't have _____ hope of _____ improvement.

5. That film is full of _____ crime and _____ violence.

D. SPELLING

Although **ea** is and a usual spelling for the sound [iy], as in *each, cheap, clean,* here are a few words in which **ea** is the spelling for the sound [ɛ]:

wealth	bread
health	dread
head	lead (*metal*)
dead	ready
read (*past tense*)	steady

E. PARAPHRASE

FORMAL	COLLOQUIAL
1. in a remote, undeveloped place	1. out in the sticks
2. were disappointed	2. had a let down
3. a tide of gold seekers flowed in	3. lots of people came looking for gold
4. having uprooted themselves	4. after they had pulled up stakes

F. IDIOMS

a great deal; a good deal = much, very much
in the tens of thousands = tens of thousands of them
build up = make greater

G. SEMANTICS

Words of related meaning:

difficulty = something hard to do; the condition of requiring much
      effort; trouble
  They had difficulty in completing the work.
hardship = something hard to bear; a painful situation
  The travelers suffered such hardships as hunger, cold, and danger of
  attack.
problem = a difficult matter which needs to be solved
  Unemployment is a serious problem.

H. COMPREHENSION

1. Who were the "Forty-niners"?
2. How did they reach California?
3. How did they search for gold?
4. Were many gold-seekers successful?
5. How did the gold rush affect the size of California's population?

I. SPEAKING AND WRITING

Discussion

1. If you had lived at that time, would you have joined in the gold rush?
2. Would you have preferred to cross the country by wagon or to sail around
   South America in order to reach California? Why?
3. Why do you suppose life was so rough there at that time?

Summary

What was the California gold rush?

16

Westward— the Great Plains

A sod house built by westward migrants in Nebraska in the 1880s. (Nebraska State Historical Society)

grant	drought
property	swarm
lack	locust
prairie	devour
sarcastic	overwhelm
marble	hardy
severe	hospitable
strenuous	

In 1862 the United States government passed a law that stimulated the settlement of the Great Plains west of the Mississippi River. This Homestead Act granted 160 acres of land to any settler who lived on it and farmed a part of it for five years. After that, the land became the settler's own property. This offer attracted land-hungry people from many places. In addition to migrants from the eastern states, many Scandinavians, Slavs, and other Europeans came, seeking land to farm.

Unlike the older frontier areas east of the Mississippi, these western plains were treeless, covered only with tall prairie grass. Because of the lack of wood, a pioneer family would build its first house of sod—dried bricks made of earth (referred to sarcastically as "prairie marble"). This area presented other problems, too. The weather was often severe, with burning summer heat and biting winter winds, and the labor of breaking the soil was strenuous. Occasionally there were long periods of drought, which ruined the crops. Some years swarms of locusts flew in like a dark cloud, settled on the fields, and devoured every green leaf. Those homesteaders who could not bear such hardships or who were overwhelmed by the strangeness of the new, empty land became discouraged and left. But the most courageous and hardy remained.

There were other pioneers who went even beyond the Great Plains. They had to cross still another barrier, the very high Rocky Mountains; but the land between the mountains and the Pacific was far more hospitable. It was all of these hardy pioneers who built up the American West.

A. PRONUNCIATION

Short **e** [ɛ] contrasts in sound with short **i** [I]. Can you clearly hear the difference? Can you pronounce these words so that people can tell which one you mean?

[ε]	*versus*	[I]
emigrant		immigrant
weather		wither
left		lift
ten		tin
tell		till
belt		built
bet		bit
red		rid
well		will
hem		him
bell		bill

B. WORD FORMATION

The adjective ending **-less** means 'without.' Some **-less** adjectives have opposites ending in **-ful**.

treeless	
heartless	
painless	painful
harmless	harmful
penniless	

C. GRAMMAR

The passive is used with impersonal meaning. The passive form consists of **be** in the right tense, plus the past participle of the verb. To focus on the *actor*, that is, the person or thing performing the action, use the active form of the verb, rather than the passive. (Note that the subject of the passive verb matches the object of the active verb.)

passive
The house was built of sod.
 Who built it?

active
The pioneer built the house.
The pioneer (did).

Note that in a short answer *do* or *did* can be a substitute for the verb or for the rest of the sentence. Here are more examples of active and passive forms.

> The crops were ruined.
> *What ruined them?*
> The drought ruined the crops.
> The drought (did).
>
> Land was given to the settlers.
> *Who gave it to them?*
> The government gave it to them.
> The government (did).
>
> The land was farmed for five years.
> *Who farmed it?*
> The homesteaders farmed it.
> The homesteaders (did).
>
> Laws are passed to encourage land settlement.
> *Who passes such laws?*
> Congress passes them.
> Congress (does).

PRACTICE EXERCISE

Make up questions beginning with *who* or *what* based on the following statements, and answer each one with full and with short sentences, using an active verb.

> Examples:
>
> The houses were destroyed.
> *What destroyed them?*
> The flood destroyed them.
> The flood (did).
>
> The play was performed in the theater.
> *Who performed it?*
> The drama club performed it.
> The drama club (did).

1. A prize is given to the winner.
2. The lost child was found.
3. A cake was baked for his birthday party.
4. A tree was planted in front of the house.
5. The room is cleaned every day.

D. SPELLING

The letter **o** followed by a consonant followed by **e** (**o**-*consonant*-**e**) is pronounced [ow]. When the consonant is **v**, however, **o** is usually pronounced [ʌ].

o pronounced [ow]	**o** pronounced [ʌ]
home	love
rode	above
stone	glove
slope	dove
hope	shove
explode	hover
bone	cover
close	shovel
cone	oven
alone	hovel
tone	
rope	
robe	

E. PARAPHRASE

FORMAL	COLLOQUIAL
1. It encouraged the westward movement.	1. It gave the westward movement a boost.
2. They lacked wood.	2. They ⎰didn't have any wood.⎱ were short of wood.
3. They could not bear the hardships.	3. They couldn't ⎰stand it.⎱ take it. ⎰stick it out.

F. IDIOMS

The word **up** is used as an intensifier for some verbs.

build up = develop; increase
burn up = burn completely; destroy by fire
buy up = buy all of them; buy all of it
tear up = tear into small pieces
finish up = finish completely

blow up = explode
shoot up = shoot wildly and repeatedly; wreck

G. SEMANTICS

Words of related meaning:

It was just a bare hut for the hunters.

cabin = small, simple country house
Thoreau built a little cabin in the woods.

home = house where a person feels he or she belongs
We like our guests to feel that this is their home.

homestead = house with farm buildings
The government encouraged the pioneers to set up homesteads in the West.

soil = ground to grow plants in
Iowa has excellent soil for growing corn.

sod = soil with grass roots, or soil cut into blocks
Because they had no wood, the pioneers used sod to build their houses.

land = stretch of ground
They used most of the land for farming.

H. COMPREHENSION

1. Who joined the American migrants?
2. Describe the Great Plains.
3. What is a sod house? Do you understand the ''prairie marble'' joke?
4. What endangered the crops?
5. Why did some migrants go back?

I. SPEAKING AND WRITING

Discussion

1. In *Giants in the Earth*, a novel written in the early 1900s by Ole Roolvag, a pioneer woman's homesickness and fears drive her insane. Is that understandable?

2. Why did the government give land to settlers? Why did it insist that they live on it and farm it?
3. Would you like to cross the Rocky Mountains? How?

Summary

Summarize the selection in two or three sentences.

17
Cowboys

The Long Drive—cowboys herding cattle on their way northward. (Denver Public Library)

cattle	identification
herd	equipment
steer (*noun*)	cope with
graze	harsh
perform	thief
duty	ranch
brand (*verb*)	

Cowboys were herders of cattle with many hard tasks to perform in dealing with large herds on the range, the open grasslands of the Middle West. They became famous in the days of the Long Drives, from about 1860 to 1886.

Every spring as the grass turned green, huge herds of Texas steers were driven north to railroad shipping centers. The drive northward covered about half ⁵ the length of the United States. As the cattle moved along, they grazed and grew heavier. From these centers the steers were shipped by rail, mostly to the Chicago market, where they were sold for about ten times their Texas price.

The cowboys' work was hard and unromantic. From dawn to dark they performed their duties, rounding up the cattle, branding them for identification, ¹⁰ and repairing equipment. A small group of cowboys had full responsibility for a herd of thousands. They had to cope with harsh weather and to protect the herd against cattle thieves, Indian fighters, and angry farmers, who feared the ruin of their crops.

In 1886 as a result of very bad weather, which caused the death of huge ¹⁵ numbers of cattle on the ''open range,'' the Long Drives were discontinued. From then on the steers had to be cared for and fattened on large ranches in the Texas area before being shipped north by rail; the cowboys now became more settled ranch workers.

Although the cowboy was not the exciting, romantic hero or villain of the ²⁰ ''western'' movies, he did play an important part in the development of the American West.

A. PRONUNCIATION

1. The plural noun ending **-s** is pronounced as a separate syllable [əz] only when it follows a sibilant. The sibilants are [s], [z], [š], [ž], [č], [j].

ranches	hedges
pages	villages
grasses	garages
bushes	notices
roses	lunches

2. After the voiceless consonants *p*, *t*, *k*, *f*, and voiceless *th*, the noun plural ending is pronounced [s]:

tasks	states	moths
crops	notes	deaths
books	migrants	
cuffs	parents	

3. In all other situations the noun plural ending **-s** is pronounced [z]:

after a voiced consonant		*after a vowel sound*
steers	herders	days
herds	farmers	ways
bags	centers	cows
thousands	grasslands	cowboys
		duties

Be especially careful with silent **e** words. The following are one-syllable words with the plural ending pronounced [z]:

1 syllable

times
thieves
drives
sides
robes

B. WORD FORMATION

Comparative form of adjectives.

1. Adjectives of one syllable (or two syllables ending in **y**) take the ending **-er** (meaning 'more so') for the comparative.

heavy	heavier
fat	fatter
slow	slower
high	higher
muddy	muddier

The cattle were heavy; they became even heavier on the Long Drive.
They were not very fat at first; but as they grazed, they became fatter.

Their progress was slow; when the weather was bad, it was even slower.
The price was not high in Texas; in Chicago it became much higher.
The paths were often muddy; when it rained, they became even muddier.

2. If the adjective is a rather long word, instead of adding **-er** to form the comparative, use the word **more** (or **less**) before the adjective.

> Cowboys became famous in the days of the Long Drive; later, the movies made them *more famous*.
> Nowadays beef is expensive; in times of inflation it becomes even *more expensive*.

PRACTICE EXERCISE

Fill in each blank with the correct (comparative) form of the adjective.

1. Tom is tall, but his big brother is even ＿＿＿＿＿＿.
   (tall)

2. That car is too small; I want to get a ＿＿＿＿＿＿ one.
   (big)

3. When there is no moon, the stars are ＿＿＿＿＿＿.
   (bright)

4. In bad weather the cowboys' work was even ＿＿＿＿＿＿.
   (difficult)

5. The ＿＿＿＿＿＿ sister helps to take care of her ＿＿＿＿＿＿ brother.
   (old)   (young)

6. Travel is ＿＿＿＿＿＿ if you know something about the place.
   (interesting)

C. GRAMMAR

In questions, **do** is used with the verb for present tense and **did** for past (unless the verb is a form of **be**). Thus a statement with the verb in the present tense matches a question with **do**, and a statement in the past tense matches a question with **did**. (Review chapter 10, section C2.)

> **Do** people still **like** cowboy stories?
> Yes, people **like** them.

Do you **like** cowboy movies?
I **like** cowboy movies.
When **did** the cowboys **drive** the cattle north?
The cowboys **drove** them north in the spring.
Why **did** the cattle **grow** heavier?
They **grew** heavier because they ate the grass.
Where **did** they **sell** the cattle?
They **sold** the cattle in Chicago.
When **did** the cowboy **begin** his daily duties?
He **began** them at dawn.
Why **did** the cattle **die**?
The cattle **died** as a result of bad weather.

If the verb (or the auxiliary) is a form of **be**, then **do** is not used, and the verb form is the same in the statement and in the question.

Were the cowboys brave?
The cowboys **were** brave.
Was the Long Drive difficult?
The Long Drive **was** difficult.
Is he a student here?
He **is** a student here.
Are they **coming** with us?
They **are coming** with us.

D. SPELLING

The regular spelling for possessive nouns adds an apostrophe and **s** to the noun for the singular; the apostrophe is placed after the **s** of the plural.

SINGULAR	PLURAL
a cowboy's work	the cowboys' Long Drive
the baby's mother	babies' diseases
the lady's pocketbook	ladies' fashions
Mr. Miller's car	the Millers' car
	(the car of the Miller family)

There is a special spelling for the possessive if the plural of the noun does not end in **s**. For such nouns **'s** is added to form plural possessive.

SINGULAR	PLURAL
the child's mother	many children's mothers
a man's wallet	many men's wallets
one sheep's wool	many sheep's wool

If a singular name ends in **s**, either **'s** is added to form the possessive, or just an apostrophe is added after the name, without another **s**.

Charles's	*or*	Charles'
Mr. Burns's	*or*	Mr. Burns'

PRACTICE EXERCISE

Change the prepositional phrase to a possessive plus a noun.

Examples:

pocketbooks for ladies — **ladies'** pocketbooks
the mother of the child — the **child's** mother
the job of William — **William's** job

1. the desk of our teacher
2. toys of the children
3. suits for men
4. the car of Mr. Jones
5. songs of birds
6. books for students
7. the phone number of Mary
8. the secretary of Dr. Smith

E. PARAPHRASE

FORMAL	COLLOQUIAL
They had many hard tasks to perform.	They had many tough jobs to do.
The drives were discontinued.	The drives were called off.

F. IDIOMS

> went on = continued, was in progress
> took place = happened
> covered ten miles = traveled a distance of ten miles
> played an important part = contributed greatly
> moved along = continued on their way

G. SEMANTICS

The group word for bovine animals is **cattle**. Some kinds of cattle are:

> steer — raised for beef
> cow — female
> bull — male
> calf — young
> ox — beast of burden

H. COMPREHENSION

1. After completing the Long Drive, how did the cattle travel the rest of the way to the markets?
2. What hardships did cowboys have on the way?
3. What were the dangers?
4. How did the cowboys' job change after the Long Drives were discontinued?

I. SPEAKING AND WRITING

Discussion

1. Why do you suppose that the Long Drive was started in the spring?
2. Why were the steers so much more expensive in Chicago than in Texas?

Summary

What kind of job did cowboys have?

18

The Buffalo
and the Plains Indians

Shooting at the buffalo as a herd crosses the train tracks. (Kansas State Historical Society)

buffalo	hide (*noun*)
bison	moccasins
bovine	prey (*verb*)
roam	crew
estimate	scarce
nomad	drastic

The buffalo, or American bison, is a large bovine which once roamed the western plains in huge herds, migrating as it ate the tall grass. It has been estimated that in the early 1800s, fifty million buffaloes existed there. The nomadic Plains Indians were dependent on the buffalo, and they kept on the move following the herds. From time to time the men would organize a group hunt, 5 chasing the animals into an enclosure or over a cliff. Some of the buffalo's meat was eaten fresh; the rest was dried for later use. The hide served many purposes. It was used as the covering for the Indians' tall, cone-shaped tents, called tepees, which offered excellent protection against bad weather, and which could quickly be folded and transported as the tribe moved. It was the women who constructed 10 the tepees and who did all the chores having to do with moving. Clothing and moccasins were also made from the hide of the buffalo. Even the bones, horns, and hair of the buffalo were used in various ways.

During the later 1800s white hunters began to prey on the buffalo. Some killed them for food to feed the large crews who built the transcontinental rail- 15 road; others, for their hides, which they sold for leather. But many hunted the animals simply for sport, even shooting at them from the window of a train as it passed a herd. In a short time the buffalo became scarce. This was one of the several factors that led to a drastic change in the way of life of the Plains Indians.

A. PRONUNCIATION

The letter **a** represents both the sound [æ] and the sound [a]. Make the contrast in pronunciation.

[æ]	[a]
grass	large
nomadic	farm
began	harm
transcontinental	hard
animal	party
as	far

[æ]	[a]
passed	car
drastic	calm
factor	star
man	what
sat	watch
cap	father

B. WORD FORMATION

Adjectives are formed from some nouns by adding the adjective ending **-ic**. The adjective is pronounced with stress on the syllable before **-ic**.

NOUN	ADJECTIVE
nomad	no**mad**ic
a**ris**tocrat	aristo**crat**ic
democrat	demo**crat**ic
base	**bas**ic
poet	po**et**ic

PRACTICE EXERCISE

Complete the sentences with the appropriate form of the words listed (whether noun or adjective).

1. The members of a _____ tribe are called _____.

2. They thought he was an _____ because his manner was _____.

3. A _____ government is the only kind that a _____ would approve of.

4. For Quakers, peace is a _____ idea.

5. You don't have to be a _____ to have _____ feelings sometimes.

C. GRAMMAR

The **-ing** word (called the participle) may refer to a noun or pronoun which comes before it. The word it refers to is often the subject of the verb.

1. The buffalo roamed in large herds. They ate the tall grass.

   The buffalo roamed in large herds, *eating* the tall grass.

2. Many hunted them for sport. They shot at them from the trains.

Many hunted them for sport, *shooting* at them from the trains.

PRACTICE EXERCISE

Combine each pair of short sentences to form one sentence by changing the verb of the second sentence into an **-ing** word. Use an arrow to relate the **-ing** word to the noun or pronoun it refers to.

Example:

The man walked slowly. He looked straight ahead.

The man walked slowly, *looking* straight ahead.

1. They checked the results. They left no careless errors.
2. The boys washed the car. They made it look almost new.
3. Mary walked down the street. She asked everyone about her lost dog.
4. Dan looked in the encyclopedia. He hoped to find the information there.
5. The children followed the parade. They sang and danced to the music of the band.

D. SPELLING

In American English the letter **o** in closed syllables is often the spelling for the [a] sound.

stop	plot	moccasins
hot	pot	shot
hollow	cot	shop
not	continent	lock

But when the letter **o** occurs before **r** in stressed syllables, it has the pronunciation [ɔ].

short	horn	sport	cord	or
transport	for	normal	lord	nor

E. PARAPHRASE

FORMAL	COLLOQUIAL
1. led to a drastic change	1. brought on a big switch
2. hunted them simply for sport	2. hunted them just for fun
3. began to prey on them	3. went after them
4. organized a group {hunt {attack	4. ganged up on them

F. IDIOMS

on the move = traveling constantly

served a purpose = was useful

which once roamed the Plains = which roamed at a time in the past, but no longer

number in the millions = amounting to millions

from time to time = at intervals; at certain times

having to do with = involved in

G. SEMANTICS

These words are somewhat similar in meaning:

calculate = determine by arithmetic

estimate = make an approximate judgment

judge = form an opinion on the basis of evidence

guess = form an opinion at random, without evidence

H. COMPREHENSION

1. Why did the Plains Indians follow the buffalo?
2. Why was the tepee a good home for the Plains Indians?
3. Name some of the products made from the buffalo.
4. How were the herds destroyed?

I. SPEAKING AND WRITING

Discussion

1. Do you know of any other nomadic people? Why do they wander?
2. How could such large, strong animals traveling in big herds be killed by the Indians, especially before the Indians had guns?
3. Is there a lesson in the fate of the buffalo, once numbering in the millions?
4. How would scarcity of buffaloes change the life of the Indians?

Summary

Briefly summarize what you have learned in this selection.

19

The Railroad
Spans the Country

The Golden Spike Ceremony at Promontory, Utah, marking the completion of the Transcontinental Railroad. (Denver Public Library, Western History Dept.)

rapid	mountain range
curiosity	transcontinental
encounter	link
troublesome	authorize
bear (*verb*)	seaboard
effective	generous
brake	subsidy
means (*noun*)	project

A rapid means of long-distance transportation became a necessity for the United States as settlement spread ever farther westward. The early trains were impractical curiosities, and for a long time the railroad companies encountered troublesome mechanical problems. The most serious ones were the construction of rails able to bear the load, and the development of a safe, effective braking system. Once these were solved, the railroad was established as the best means of land transportation. By 1860 there were thousands of miles of track crossing the eastern mountain ranges and reaching westward to the Mississippi. There were also regional southern and western lines.

The high point in railroad building came with the construction of the first transcontinental system. In 1862 Congress authorized two western railroad companies to build lines from Nebraska westward and from California eastward to a meeting point, so as to complete a transcontinental crossing linking the Atlantic seaboard with the Pacific. The government helped the railroads generously with subsidies and grants of land. Actual work on this project began four years later. The Central Pacific Company, starting from California, used Chinese workers, while the Union Pacific employed crews of Irish immigrants. The two groups worked at remarkable speed, each trying to cover a greater distance than the other. In 1869 they met at a place called Promontory in what is now the state of Utah. Many visitors came there for the great occasion. At the official ceremony a silver hammer was used to drive a golden spike, thus completing the union of the two railroads, while the newly-developed telegraph broadcast the announcement to the whole United States. There were joyous celebrations all over the country, with parades and the ringing of church bells to honor the great achievement.

The railroad was very important in encouraging westward migration. It also helped build up industry and farming by moving raw materials and by distributing products rapidly to distant markets. In linking towns and people to one another it helped unify the United States.

A. PRONUNCIATION

The sound [ər] has several different spellings. Practice pronouncing the [ər] sound in the following words.

early	la**ter**
en**co**un**tered**	la**bor**
were	**work**ed
trans**por**tation	grea**ter**
east**ern**	visit**ors**
south**ern**	ham**mer**
first	**hon**or
author**ized**	en**cour**age
gene**rously**	a**nother**

B. WORD FORMATION

-ous is an adjective ending. Some **-ous** adjectives have a related noun, as shown in parentheses.

generous	joyous (joy)
serious	dangerous (danger)
gorgeous	mountainous (mountain)
curious	hazardous (hazard)
delicious	glorious (glory)
tremendous	nervous (nerve)
various	glamorous (glamor)

C. GRAMMAR

The "empty" **there** (see chapter 8, section C).

> There was a brake problem.
> By 1860 there were thousands of miles of track.
> There were also regional lines.
> There was an official ceremony.
> There were joyous celebrations.
> There had never been such excitement before.

PRACTICE EXERCISE

Make up sentences using the "empty" **there** with the subjects that follow on page 108. Underline the subject with one line and the verb with two lines. Remember that the **be** verb must match the subject in number—whether singular or plural.

Examples:

Present tense
  books in the library
    There <u>are</u> a thousand <u>books</u> in the library.

Past tense
  a terrible accident
    There <u>was</u> a terrible <u>accident</u> at the corner.

Present tense

1. a new <u>railroad</u>
2. many <u>miles</u> of track
3. tall <u>buildings</u> at the center of the city
4. a <u>railroad station</u> nearby
5. also a <u>bus station</u>

Past tense

1. Irish <u>immigrants</u> on the Union Pacific lines
2. Chinese <u>laborers</u> in the West
3. a <u>race</u> between them
4. a great <u>celebration</u>
5. <u>church bells</u> ringing
6. an official <u>ceremony</u>

D. SPELLING

Two of the spellings for the sound [iy] are **ie** and **ei**. To learn when to write **ie** and when to write **ei**, children memorize the rule: "*i* before *e*, except after *c*."

ie	**ei**
achieve	receive
brief	deceive
believe	conceit
piece	perceive
chief	ceiling
niece	
relief	
thief	

E. PARAPHRASE

FORMAL	COLLOQUIAL
1. A rapid means of transportation became a necessity.	1. Fast transport was needed.
2. They encountered troublesome mechanical problems.	2. They hit some snags.
3. The most serious was the construction of rails able to bear the load.	3. The toughest was getting rails strong enough for the weight.
4. The railroad encouraged westward migration.	4. The railroad gave the move west a boost.

F. IDIOMS

once these were solved = after and as a result of their being solved
ever farther westward = moving more and more to the west
build up = increase; make more successful
to one another = each one to the other(s)

G. SEMANTICS

effect (*noun*) = consequence; result produced
effective = serving the purpose; doing the job
affect (*verb*) = to produce an effect upon
efficient = performing well
effectual = producing the intended result

H. COMPREHENSION

1. What were the big problems that had to be solved to make the railroad successful?
2. What did the government encourage the railroad lines to do?
3. What great event was celebrated in Utah in 1869?
4. What was done at the ceremony?
5. How did the railroad affect the development of the United States?

I. SPEAKING AND WRITING

Discussion

1. Why would it be difficult to work out a good braking system for a railroad train?
2. Would a transcontinental railroad have been achieved if there had not been such a cooperative effort?
3. Would you have liked to see the celebration at Promontory? Why?

Summary

Summarize briefly what you learned about the railroad.

20

The Indians:
Search for a Solution

Indian woman erecting teepees. (Ewing Galloway, New York)

encroach	right (*verb*)
reduce	funds
tract	intention
Indian reservation	accustomed
injustice	adapt
champion (*verb*)	aspect
focus (*verb*)	profitable
plight	utilities

As people moved westward beyond the Mississippi, they continually encroached upon the vast lands of the various Indian tribes. These huge areas in which the Indians hunted and wandered seemed empty and unused. The pioneers saw them as places for mining, for cattle-raising, and for farming, and kept exerting pressure on the United States government to grant them some of this territory. The government then made several new treaties with the Indians, which reduced their original lands to smaller tracts called reservations. Within these smaller areas it was difficult to maintain many of their customs.

Toward the end of the nineteenth century there arose a number of organizations which were opposed to this injustice and which championed the cause of the Indians. Several writers focused on their plight and on the moral obligation of the United States to right the wrong that was done to them.

One attempt to deal with the problem was the Dawes Act of 1887. This divided the reservation lands into homesteads of 160 acres, each given to an Indian family. Congress also granted the Indians funds for education, which was to be compulsory. Unfortunately these well-intentioned programs did not work out. The Indians were accustomed to common ownership of tribal lands and to tribal units rather than to independent family living, and most of them had never been farmers. A new law passed in 1934 was somewhat better adapted to Indian customs and needs. It established self-government of communities on Indian lands, though they still remained under the supervision of the Bureau of Indian Affairs.

Today about half of the Indian population still live on reservations; the rest live in cities. All American Indians in the United States have had citizenship since 1924, but life has not improved for many of them who are very poor. After long silence, Indian groups have begun in recent years to demand control over their schools and over other aspects of their life.

Recently there has been in a number of Indian tribes an awakening to the opportunities of modern business that may lead to their economic independence. Large sums of money won in lawsuits against state governments (for Indian lands taken from them long ago) have been invested in profitable utilities and other businesses. Also, in 1987 the federal government began funding the special education of some Indian students who will return to the reservation and use what they have learned to improve the community. It is hoped that these developments will lead to a better life for Native Americans—as many Indians prefer to be called. 35

A. PRONUNCIATION

Practice pronouncing the [ʌ] sound, which occurs in closed syllables and is spelled **u**, **o**, or **ou**. The [ʌ] sound contrasts with the [a] sound in the pairs of words below.

[ʌ]	*versus*	[a]
cup		cop
luck		lock
come		calm
sum; some		psalm
cut		cot
nut		knot, not

Some more words for practicing the [ʌ] sound:

unmolested	begun
unlawful	other
injustice	fun
number	but
funds	up
compulsory	sun; son
unfortunately	such
accustomed	love
custom	money
government	rough
under	tough

B. WORD FORMATION

The prefix **un-** meaning "not" is attached at the beginning of an adjective or adverb to make its meaning negative.

unhappily	**un**clean
unlawfully	**un**real
unfortunately	**un**true
unaccustomed	**un**able
unmolested	**un**seen

C. GRAMMAR

Using a relative clause beginning with **which** is one way of combining statements. **Which** as a relative pronoun begins a clause that tells something about a noun that precedes **which** in the sentence. That noun represents something which is not human.

1. The tribes were settled on reservations. The reservations had been set aside for them.

   The tribes were settled on reservations which had been set aside for them.
2. Congress granted funds for education. Education was to be compulsory.

   Congress granted funds for education, which . . .
3. They live on Indian lands. The lands are supervised by the Bureau of Indian Affairs.

   They live on lands which . . .

PRACTICE EXERCISE

Combine each pair of short sentences into one sentence using a **which** clause. Draw an arrow to highlight the noun that **which** refers to.

Example:

A new law was passed. The law was better adapted to Indian needs.

A new law was passed, which was better adapted to Indian needs.

1. Yesterday I saw a show. It was very interesting.
2. Tom borrowed the car. The car belongs to his roommate.
3. She is taking a course. The course deals with politics.
4. John was looking for the newspaper. The newspaper was on the curb.

D. SPELLING

Don't confuse these pairs of words; they are pronounced alike but are spelled differently.

passed = moved beyond
past = in earlier time

right = correct
write = put words on paper

son = male child
sun = center of the solar system

their = belonging to them
there = in that place

knot = tangle
not = negative

some = a few; a quantity
sum = total

PRACTICE EXERCISE

Complete the sentences using the word pairs just reviewed.

1. As they walked, they _____ the house where the family had lived in _____ years.

2. John is the _____ of Mr. and Mrs. Miller.

3. He tried hard, but he could _____ untie the _____ in the string.

4. You must _____ the _____ answer to the question.

5. _____ car was right _____ in the garage.

6. We added up all the expenses to get the exact _____.

7. _____ people always arrive on time.

E. PARAPHRASE

FORMAL	COLLOQUIAL
1. continually encroached upon	1. $\begin{cases} \text{kept making inroads on} \\ \text{kept overstepping on} \end{cases}$
2. The Indians were unlawfully deprived of their land.	2. Some people $\begin{cases} \text{swiped} \\ \text{grabbed} \end{cases}$ Indian land.
3. There arose organizations opposed to this injustice.	3. Some outfits started up, taking a stand against this $\begin{cases} \text{dirty trick.} \\ \text{foul play.} \end{cases}$
4. championed their cause	4. $\begin{cases} \text{took their part} \\ \text{stood up for them} \end{cases}$

F. IDIOMS

to right the wrong = to correct the injustice
in the attempt to _____ = trying to _____
work out (well) = be successful
   (usually applies to plans rather than to persons)
take a stand = adopt an opinion or a point of view, for or against
stand up for = defend an idea or principle
take his part = defend a person

G. SEMANTICS

The following words are of similar meaning:

object' = express an opinion opposing
oppose = act or speak against
criticize = make a judgment about; find fault with
blame = lay responsibiliity for a fault or an error on someone

H. COMPREHENSION

1. What injustice was done to the Indians?
2. Who brought their plight to the attention of the public?
3. What was wrong with the Dawes Act?
4. How was the later law an improvement?
5. What new steps are being taken to improve the situation of American Indians?

I. SPEAKING AND WRITING

Discussion

1. Do you know what is meant by the expression, "The pen is mightier than the sword"? How did that apply to the situation of the Indians in the last years of the nineteenth century?
2. How can a government avoid mistakes like the plan of the Dawes Act?
3. Citizenship is important, but is it enough for people?

Summary

Briefly tell what you learned about the Indian reservations.

21

The Waves
of Immigration

Immigrants crowded on a steamship crossing the Atlantic Ocean in 1906. (Library of Congress, E. Levick)

oppress	absorb
origin	predecessor
displace	custom
Industrial Revolution	tend
flee	opponent
poverty	quota
refugee	restrict
eagerly	prejudicial

For over three centuries the United States has been the Promised Land for the oppressed and the hungry of Europe and of other parts of the world. Immigration here has come in waves, reflecting unhappy conditions in the immigrants' country of origin.

After the early periods of settlement, the first sharp increase in immigration took place in the 1830s and 1840s, bringing North European craftspeople displaced by the Industrial Revolution, and then a great influx of Irish fleeing from the dreadful poverty of the Potato Famine. German political refugees arrived shortly after. Many immigrants from northern and western Europe settled on farms in the Middle West. The Irish and others were eagerly absorbed as construction laborers on roads, bridges, and railroads as well as in factories. Most of them remained in the northern cities.

In the 1880s a tremendous tide of immigrants began coming in, this time largely from southern and eastern Europe. To most Americans these newcomers seemed far more strange than their predecessors. Their languages, customs, and ways of life were very different from those of established Americans. The newcomers moved into the poorest neighborhoods of the large cities and tended to stay together in local ghettos and to cling to their old ways. Being poor, and accustomed to poverty, they were willing to work for very low wages. This made other workers, especially those in labor unions, afraid that the immigrants would thus lower wage levels and take jobs away from Americans. Indeed, organized labor became one of the chief opponents of continued immigration. This opposition finally led to the immigration quota acts of the 1920s, which restricted further immigration, particularly from southern and eastern Europe. In 1965 these prejudicial laws were replaced by a new immigration act, which granted equal opportunity to foreigners, regardless of their place of origin. Asians, especially Koreans and Filipinos, then began to arrive, followed by Vietnamese at the end of the U.S.–Vietnam conflict. Many of these newcomers have worked very hard to establish themselves in their new land.

In the late 1970s and the 1980s, immigration from Mexico and from Central America increased greatly. In ever-growing numbers many of these immigrants simply walked across the very long common border between the United

States and Mexico. It was primarily to control this wave of immigration that the Immigration Reform Act was passed in 1986.

A. PRONUNCIATION

The "long **o**" is pronounced as the vowel [o] followed by the glide [w]. Practice this [ow] sound in the following words.

quota	those	low	road
old	home	know	boat
go	stone	flow	coat
no	phone	blow	load
cold	cone	snow	oak

How many words can you add to this list?

B. WORD FORMATION

The large majority of English verbs are regular in the way the past-time verb is formed. They add **-ed** to the present form to make the one-word past as well as the past participle (the form used after *have, has, had*).

PRESENT	ONE-WORD PAST	PAST PARTICIPLE
call	call**ed**	(have) call**ed**
play	play**ed**	(has) play**ed**
visit	visit**ed**	(had) visit**ed**

However, many of the most commonly used verbs are irregular; for example,

PRESENT	ONE-WORD PAST	PAST PARTICIPLE
come	came	(have) come
go	went	(has) gone
do	did	(had) done

PRACTICE EXERCISE

Fill in the blanks with the appropriate form of the irregular verb.

The immigrants had c____ from lands of poverty. They c____ to the Promised Land like others who had d____ so in earlier years. They

_____ (go) to live in neighborhoods where people from their old country had g____ before. They d____ this because they were homesick.

C. GRAMMAR

Nouns and adjectives after the verbs **be**, **become**, or **seem** refer to the subject of that verb.

The United States has been the Promised Land.

Some Germans were refugees.

PRACTICE EXERCISE

Underline the subject and the noun or adjective that follows the verb. Show by an arrow that the noun or adjective refers back to the subject.

Example:

The quota laws were unfair.

1. The newcomers were homesick.
2. The Irish had become construction workers.
3. These newcomers seemed strange to many Americans.
4. The immigrants have become citizens.
5. Many immigrants became farmers.
6. The cities are crowded.
7. The situation seems better.

D. SPELLING

The noun ending **-man** is changed to the spelling **-men** for plural nouns. Both the singular and plural are pronounced the same [mən] because this ending is never stressed.

SINGULAR	PLURAL
craftsman	craftsmen
workman	workmen

SINGULAR	PLURAL
gentleman	gentlemen
policeman	policemen
postman	postmen
congressman	congressmen

E. PARAPHRASE

FORMAL	COLLOQUIAL
1. reflecting unhappy conditions in their country of origin	1. because it was tough back home
2. the first sharp increase	2. the first big $\begin{cases} \text{jump} \\ \text{boost} \end{cases}$
3. a tremendous tide began coming in	3. loads of them began pouring in
4. tended to stay together	4. stuck together
5. restricted further immigration	5. held immigration down
6. regardless of their land of origin	6. no matter where they came from

F. IDIOMS

country of origin = place they came from
shortly after = a short time later
in ever-growing numbers = more and more of them

G. SEMANTICS

Words of related meaning:

influx = coming in like a stream
tide = periodic rise (and fall) of water of the ocean

restrict = hold within limits
restrain = hold back; control
limit = set bounds or limits to

H. COMPREHENSION

1. Which group of immigrants came first? Why did they come?
2. Why did the Irish come, and what jobs did they fill?

3. How were the immigrants of the 1880s and later different from their predecessors?
4. Who feared them and why?
5. From what faraway places do many of the newer immigrants come?

I. SPEAKING AND WRITING

Discussion

1. Although immigrants from different places were different in certain ways, what did they all have in common (how were they alike)?
2. Do "insiders" tend to object to "outsiders" who come to live among them or near them? Why?

Summary

Briefly summarize what you learned about immigration to the United States.

22

The Yankee Peddler

A wagon peddler showing his goods to settlers of the West.

peddler	arrange
colony	item
link	inexpensive
settle	ailment
welcome	shore
arrival	successful
barter	eventually

The Yankee peddler played a part in American life, from the early days of the colonies until the last years of the nineteenth century. Although not all the peddlers were "Yankees," this name was used because many of them—especially at first—came from the New England states, whose inhabitants are called Yankees. For communities far from large cities the peddler was a link with   5
the outside world. Everywhere he was welcome for the goods he brought, as well as for his news and gossip. In small, out-of-the-way settlements his arrival was an exciting event. In earlier days and with poorer customers, the peddler sometimes bartered instead of selling for money. He would trade his goods for farm products or handmade articles.   10

Some peddlers traveled from place to place on foot, carrying their stock in a trunk or a cloth bag on their backs. In order to crowd as much as possible into so little space, they arranged the articles very cleverly, fitting them carefully into one another. They brought fabrics, sewing supplies, and other small manufac-tured items.   15

Those peddlers who were lucky enough to have a wagon added bulkier goods to their stock—pots and pans, hats, shoes, even books. When inexpensive clocks began to be manufactured, they were favored items, and so were medicines that claimed to be a cure for almost any ailment. Along the Mississippi River there were peddlers who traveled in small boats loaded with their goods, stopping   20
at the settlements near the shore.

Some of the peddlers later became successful merchants, and a few of them eventually established big department stores and other large-scale busi-nesses. A peddler named Adam Gimbel set up a store called Gimbel Brothers in a town in Indiana, then branched out to Milwaukee, Philadelphia, New York, San   25
Francisco, and other cities. The great-grandfather of Senator Barry Goldwater likewise began as a peddler, then settled down in Phoenix, Arizona to found what is now Goldwaters, Inc.; Marshall Field's, Altman's, and the well-known Indi-anapolis store, L.S. Ayers, had similar beginnings.

Perhaps the most interesting story of peddler success is that of Levi   30
Strauss, a peddler who traveled from New York by clipper ship to sell needles, thread, and blue denim tent-cloth to the gold-seekers of California in 1849. While pushing his loaded cart over a muddy road in San Francisco, he met a Forty-niner

who said that what he needed was not tent cloth but tough trousers to replace the badly torn ones that he was wearing. This led to the making of the first pair of denim Levis (also called *jeans* or *dungarees*), now worn all over the world.

35

A. PRONUNCIATION

The sounds [m], [b], and [p] are called bilabial because they are produced by the two lips. In English bilabial sounds are pronounced with tight closing of the lips.

Practice saying [m]

welcome	remain
almost	customer
sometimes	community
them	small
items	ailment
claimed	settlement
farm	arrangement

Make a clear difference between the words in he following pairs. The lips do not close for the [n] sound.

[m]	*versus*	[n]
sum		sun
comb		cone
them		then
seem		seen
foam		phone

Practice saying [b]

bag	able
about	label
fabrics	table
barter	rubber

Make a clear difference between the words in the following pairs. The lower lip touches the upper teeth for the [v] sound.

[b]	*versus*	[v]
ban		van
boat		vote
berry		very
best		vest
bat		vat

Practice saying [p]

peddler	**p**ans
s**p**ace	o**p**en
u**p**	ex**p**ensive
pots	re**p**lace

B. WORD FORMATION

Nouns with the suffix **-ment** are often based on related verbs.

VERB	NOUN
settle	settlement
ail ('be sick')	ailment
arrange	arrangement
refresh	refreshment
establish	establishment
enjoy	enjoyment

C. GRAMMAR

In negative sentences with verbs that have auxiliaries, **not** comes after the auxiliary (after the first auxiliary, if there is more than one). Note that the **-n't** contraction of **not** is attached to the auxiliary. With **am** no contraction of **not** is used.

The peddler $\begin{Bmatrix} \text{was not} \\ \text{wasn't} \end{Bmatrix}$ traveling on foot.

He $\begin{Bmatrix} \text{can not} \\ \text{cannot} \\ \text{can't} \end{Bmatrix}$ carry such heavy articles.

He $\begin{Bmatrix} \text{has not} \\ \text{hasn't} \end{Bmatrix}$ been seen here.

This medicine $\begin{Bmatrix} \text{will not} \\ \text{won't} \end{Bmatrix}$ cure his disease.

If the customer $\begin{Bmatrix} \text{could not} \\ \text{couldn't} \end{Bmatrix}$ pay cash,

the peddler $\begin{Bmatrix} \text{would not} \\ \text{wouldn't} \end{Bmatrix}$ refuse to do business with him.

The contraction of **I am** is **I'm**:

$\begin{Bmatrix} \text{I am not going there.} \\ \text{I'm not going there.} \end{Bmatrix}$

PRACTICE EXERCISE

Change the following sentences from the positive to the negative form.

Examples:

We have been away from home.

We $\begin{Bmatrix} \text{have not} \\ \text{haven't} \end{Bmatrix}$ been away from home.

They are expecting him today.

They $\begin{Bmatrix} \text{are not} \\ \text{aren't} \end{Bmatrix}$ expecting him today.

1. Fine, handmade clocks were sold by the peddler.
2. If the customer could pay cash, the peddler would do business with him.
3. This peddler traveled in a small boat.
4. He has stopped at settlements along the shore.
5. He can trade his goods for farm products.
6. His grandfather was a peddler.

D. SPELLING

Here are more words that sound alike but have different meanings and different spellings.

its—belonging to it
it's—it is

so—in that manner; to such an extent
sew—make with needle and thread

to—a preposition; begins the infinitive (*to go*, *to see*, *to do*, etc.)
too—also; more than enough
two—the number 2

know—be aware of: be acquainted with
no—negative

see—observe by looking
sea—large body of water

for—a preposition
four—the number 4

wood—from a tree
would—auxiliary verb

PRACTICE EXERCISE

Complete the sentences using the correct words from the list above.

1. We must hurry; _____ late!
     (its, it's)

2. I asked her to _____ it for me. I don't _____ _____
                  (so, sew)   (so, sew)   (to, too, two)
   well.

3. One of these is enough; _____ would be _____ many.
                           (to, too, two)   (to, too, two)

4. They speak only Spanish; they _____ _____ English.
                                 (know, no) (know, no)

5. He lives at the shore; he can _____ the _____ from his
                                 (see, sea)   (see, sea)
   window.

6. I asked _____ _____ of them, but he gave me only three.
           (for, four) (for, four)

7. We _____ buy _____ there for our fireplace.
     (wood, would)   (wood, would)

E. PARAPHRASE

FORMAL	COLLOQUIAL
1. to crowd so much into so little space	1. to $\begin{Bmatrix} \text{squeeze} \\ \text{get} \end{Bmatrix}$ it all in
2. They were favored items.	2. People $\begin{Bmatrix} \text{wanted} \\ \text{went for} \end{Bmatrix}$ them.
3. They eventually established stores.	3. Later they set up stores.
4. medicines that were claimed to be a cure for any ailment	4. cure-alls

F. IDIOMS

out-of-the-way = remote; isolated
and so were they = and they were, too

branch out = expand, extend—often used of business or other activities
settle down = become established, stay
make use of = use for one's own purposes, employ

G. SEMANTICS

Words of related meaning:

peddler = traveling seller of small merchandise, at retail
vendor = one who sells on the street
merchant = one who sells for profit, and owns his or her business or store
salesperson = one who is employed to sell goods

sell = give something, for money
buy = get something by paying for it
exchange = give up something for something else
trade = buy and sell, or exchange goods
barter = trade by exchanging goods, not by using money

H. COMPREHENSION

1. Where did the peddler go?
2. Why were people glad to see him?
3. What did he sell?
4. How did peddlers travel?
5. What did some peddlers finally do?

I. SPEAKING AND WRITING

Discussion

1. What qualities of character do you suppose a peddler had to have? Why?
2. Why do you suppose long-distance peddling ended in the late years of the nineteenth century?
3. Is barter a good way to do business? Why or why not?
4. What do you suppose the isolated settlers did to tell time, before the inexpensive clocks were available?

Summary

Briefly tell what you learned about the peddler.

23

Educating the Young

Chemistry laboratory students at Bartram High School, Philadelphia, "learn by doing." (Joel DiBartolomeo)

support	compulsory
faith	attendance
essential	youth
promote	diversified
entitle	preparation
authorities	vocation
standards	accelerated

As early as 1647 Massachusetts had a law ruling that free, tax-supported schools must be established in every town having fifty households or more. Americans have always had great faith in education. They believe that in a democracy all citizens must have some education in order to understand economic and political matters and to vote wisely. They also believe that education is 5 essential to progress and prosperity; that public education promotes equality; and that every person is entitled to as much education as he or she can absorb.

The public schools of the United States are not controlled by the national government nor by church authorities but by the local communities themselves, with state laws setting educational standards and ruling on compulsory atten- 10 dance.

Among the most active in establishing free public education were the labor unions. From the 1830s on, public school systems developed, starting in the northeastern states and gradually spreading to the other parts of the country. In addition to public schools there are also various private and religious schools. 15

By 1986, seventy-six percent of the youth were graduating from high school, and almost half of these were beginning college or other post–high school study. With so much of the population attending school, education is necessarily diversified, to meet the students' various needs. Besides courses for college preparation, there are many kinds of commercial and vocational training. Stu- 20 dents are also allowed a choice of subjects. Methods of teaching vary widely, too. In addition there are specialized public schools for the handicapped and for those with other special needs, as well as accelerated and enriched courses for gifted students.

American schools are equipped with a large variety of learning aids, 25 including audio–visual equipment, language laboratories, closed-circuit television, computers, science laboratories, and an assortment of industrial arts shops.

Ever since the beginning of this century, American education has been under the influence of the ideas of the philosopher John Dewey, who believed that education should be a preparation for life, that a person learns by doing, and that 30 teaching must stimulate the curiosity and the creativity of children and youth.

A. PRONUNCIATION

[š]	versus	[č]
shop		church
vacation		choice
rush		such
special		children
sheep		cheap
ship		chip
shoe		chew
shin		chin
shore		chore
sheer		cheer

B. WORD FORMATION

The noun ending **-ity** means 'state' or 'condition'. The stress is always on the syllable before the **-ity** ending.

prosperity	condition of being	prosperous
creativity	" " "	creative
curiosity	" " "	curious
diversity	" " "	diverse
jollity	" " "	jolly

C. GRAMMAR

The present perfect tense (**have_____ed**) indicates an action (or condition) that began in the past and continues into the present (or still has consequences in the present).

For many generations Americans have had faith in education.
   (They did, and they still do.)
For many generations Americans had faith in education.
   (They did, but not any longer.)
I have lived in Chicago for ten years.
   (I still live in Chicago.)
I lived in Chicago for ten years.
   (I no longer live there.)

He has done business here often.
  (He does to this day.)
He did business here often.
  (He did in the past but not now.)

Adverbs that are often used with the present perfect tense include *just*, *already*, *recently*, *often*, *never*, *not* . . . *yet*, as well as phrases beginning with *since*. The present perfect is *not* used with terms indicating specific past time, such as *yesterday*, *last year*, *a week ago*, *on March 5*, *in 1950*.

PRACTICE EXERCISE

In each sentence select the present perfect tense of the verb or the one-word past tense and explain your choice.

Examples:

The mechanic *has* just *finished* the job. (by now; "just")
He *phoned* us last week. (specific past time, "last week")
Americans *have* always *celebrated* Thanksgiving. (and they still do)

1. I _____ music all my life.
   (love)

2. Suddenly he _____ and _____.
   (slip)   (fall)

3. The plane _____ there by now.
   (arrive)

4. He _____ here a few years ago.
   (work)

5. Mary _____ in 1982.
   (graduate)

6. This always _____ the custom here, and it still is.
   (be)

7. They _____ away last month.
   (move)

8. His parents _____ him this watch last Christmas.
   (give)

9. We _____ good friends all this time.
   (be)

10. Yesterday we _____ a long walk in the park.
    (take)

D. SPELLING

The sound [š] can be spelled in several ways. The regular spelling is **sh**:

shell	**sh**out
hu**sh**	cra**sh**

Note the special spellings **ti** and **ci**:

na**ti**on	spe**ci**al	gla**ci**er
nutri**ti**ous	ra**ci**al	an**ci**ent
por**ti**on	spa**ci**ous	
cau**ti**ous	atro**ci**ous	

Note also the spelling **ssi** in such words as mi**ssi**on, emi**ssi**on, fi**ssi**on, and **s** before **u** (sugar, sure, insure, censure, erasure).

E. PARAPHRASE

FORMAL	COLLOQUIAL
1. have always had faith in	1. have always believed in
2. Education is essential to progress and prosperity.	2. You can't get ahead without education.
3. Among the most active in establishing free public education were the labor unions.	3. The labor unions did most to start free public schools.
4. Students are allowed a choice of subjects.	4. Students can pick their subjects.

F. IDIOMS

as early as = beginning with the time
ever since = from that time on; from that time to now
under the influence of = influenced by
in addition (to) = besides; also

G. SEMANTICS

Like most words, the verb **promote** has several meanings, including:

advance or encourage the development of something
Public education promotes the welfare of the people.

raise in rank or position
Ms. Smith was promoted to the vice-presidency of the company.
put ahead to the next grade in school
Since he passed all his subjects, he was promoted.

Similarly, the noun **authority** has several meanings:

the right to control or command
The manager has the authority to hire or fire workers.
a person or group having such a right
They appealed to the authorities.
a recognized, accepted source of information
Jones is an authority on classical music.

H. COMPREHENSION

1. What has been the attitude toward education in the United States?
2. Who controls education in the United States?
3. Why is it necessary to have diversified education?
4. How advanced is educational equipment in the United States?
5. What were Dewey's ideas about education?

I. SPEAKING AND WRITING

Discussion

1. Is the character of American education aristocratic or democratic? How?
2. Why would the labor unions have been eager to establish free public school systems?
3. Why would the most industrialized part of the country have been first in public education?

Summary

Briefly summarize what you learned about public education in the United States.

24

Higher Education

Harvard University in 1828, almost 200 years after it was founded. (Library of Congress)

existence	liberal education
ordinance	tenfold
encourage	available
agricultural	tuition
technical	enroll
gradually	minority
coeducation	blacks
support	recruit (*verb*)

Only a few years after the Pilgrims set foot on American soil, Harvard College was established, in 1634. Eight more colleges were already in existence before the Revolutionary War. The Land Ordinance of 1785, opening a large area between the Ohio and Mississippi Rivers for settlement, set aside one-sixteenth of the land to cover the expenses of public education. A further rule of Congress   5
stated that "schools and the means of education shall forever be encouraged." Later the Morrill Act of 1862 gave a large piece of land to each state so that the profit from that land would pay for establishing agricultural and technical colleges. Many of these state colleges have since grown into large universities.

In the early nineteenth century a number of colleges for women were   10
founded. Gradually colleges for men only began to admit women, and many colleges and universities have become coeducational.

A number of important technical colleges were founded at the beginning of this century, including the world-famous California Institute of Technology and Massachusetts Institute of Technology.   15

Today we have a great variety of types of colleges and universities in the United States. Some are state-supported, others are privately endowed, and still others are supported by religious sects. Some of these institutions focus on a general liberal education; others on technical and practical training, on specialized research, on the fine arts, or on preparation for the practice of a profession.   20
Between 1900 and 1950 college enrollment multiplied tenfold, and it has grown much greater since then. The students represent all economic levels of society and all races.

State governments and other governmental agencies, special foundations, and the colleges themselves grant many scholarships to students with special   25
abilities and to those with financial needs. And the federal government has established a large-scale program offering long-term loans to students to help them meet their educational expenses. The goal is to make higher education available to everyone who is willing and capable—regardless of his or her financial situation.

To spread educational opportunity to more of the population, new kinds   30
of colleges have been established. These include community colleges, two-year junior colleges, and evening courses aimed at meeting the needs of daytime

workers. There are city-supported and state-supported colleges that charge little or no tuition. Some of them have an open-admissions policy that allows anyone who has graduated from high school to attend. ⁣35

Many colleges and universities have been making special efforts to enroll more minority students, especially blacks. Representatives recruit minority students, and often offer them special financial and instructional help when needed. Many foreign students come to the United States, some supported by the U.S. government's Institute of International Education or by other American institutions or foundations. Academic opportunity and achievement have always been and still are an important part of American life. The United States can be proud of its democratic educational heritage. ⁣40

A. PRONUNCIATION

Practice the vowel sound [ey], pronouncing the [y] glide.

education	today
stated	training
later	preparation
gave	great
state	race
pay	agency
male	foundation

Contrast the [ey] sound with the [ɛ] by saying each pair in the following list.

[ey]	versus	[ɛ]
fail		fell
sale		sell
tale		tell
main		men
late		let
raid		red
trade		tread
gate		get
wait		wet
mate		met
jail		jell

B. WORD FORMATION

Prepositions beginning with **be-** indicate position.

> **before** = preceding in time; preceding in pace
> The house was built before the Revolutionary War.
> He stood before me in the line.
> **behind** = back of; after
> The garage is behind the house.
> **below** = in a lower place
> Fish swim below the surface of the water.
> **beneath** = under something
> **beside** = alongside; next to
> **between** = in the space (or time) separating two things
> **beyond** = more than; farther than

PRACTICE EXERCISE

Use each of the **be-** prepositions in a sentence. Underline each prepositional phrase. (Remember that a prepositional phrase does not have a verb in it.)

> Example:
>
> He felt nervous, standing *before the large audience.*

C. GRAMMAR

Many common one-syllable verbs make a special combination with certain adverbial particles: **up, down, out, off, over, through, along, around, aside, by, in, on,** and others. If the object of the verb is a noun, it is placed either after or between the two parts. If the object is a pronoun, it must come between them. (When the object comes between, the particle is stressed.)

> **set aside** part of the land
> **set** part of the land **aside**
> set it **aside**   (*not* set aside it)

> **sent out** representatives
> **sent** representatives **out**
> sent them **out**   (*not* sent out them)

bring up a child
bring a child **up**
bring her **up**   (*not* bring up her)

shouted down his opponent
shouted his opponent **down**
shouted him **down**   (*not* shouted down him)

took away the package
took the package **away**
took it **away**   (*not* took away it)

PRACTICE EXERCISE

Make up expressions using each of the following verb-particle combinations with an appropriate object. Write each expression using a noun in both positions and then a pronoun.

Example:

set up (establish)
    set up a business
    set a business up
    set it up

1. bring about (cause, make something happen)
2. call off (cancel a plan or an event)
3. figure out (calculate, succeed in understanding)
4. find out (discover, learn by investigating)
5. keep up (continue, maintain)
6. put off (delay to a later time)
7. try out (test something)
8. turn down (reject)
9. wipe out (destroy, kill off)
10. call up (contact by telephone)

D. SPELLING

A special, irregular spelling of [ey] is **eigh**.

eight	freight	sleigh
weight	neighbor	

E. PARAPHRASE

FORMAL	COLLOQUIAL
1. Eight more colleges were already in existence.	1. There were already eight more colleges.
2. a great variety of types of colleges	2. lots of different kinds of colleges
3. College enrollment multiplied tenfold.	3. Ten times as many people went to college.
4. to make education available to more people	4. to give more people a chance for education

F. IDIOMS

set foot on = arrive at
cover the expenses of = pay for
meet their educational expenses = pay for their education

G. SEMANTICS

Words of related meaning:

Ordinance, **law**, and **regulation** are synonyms meaning a kind of rule.
An **ordinance** is a formal rule established by a government or a religious authority.
A **law** is a written rule or decree passed by a government.
A **regulation** is an order for controlling behavior, usually dealing with details or small matters.

H. COMPREHENSION

1. When in American history did higher education begin?
2. How was education provided for in the westward migration?
3. What types of colleges and universities can be found in the United States today?
4. What is being done about the minorities?

I. SPEAKING AND WRITING

Discussion

1. Most of the American colleges and universities which were originally for men only have begun admitting women, and women's colleges have opened their doors to men. Do you think that this is a wise change?
2. Why do you suppose the federal government has particularly encouraged technical and agricultural education?
3. Do you agree with the policy of giving special financial help and educational assistance to minority students?

Summary

In two or three sentences, summarize the information in this reading selection.

25

The General Store
and
the Country Auction

Country auction near Ellenville, New York, in April 1982. (Ken Karp)

mail-order
mall
auction
pot-bellied stove
produce (*noun*)
patent medicine
prosper
equipment

hardware
implement (*noun*)
local
bid
patter
gruff
ridicule

In this land of department stores, mail-order catalogues, supermarkets, and shopping malls, there remain two old-fashioned, rural styles of shopping: the general store and the country auction. The general store is an old institution. In the farm village, the frontier settlement, or the small town, the general store was a place to exchange gossip and to argue politics by the dim light of oil lamps. In winter, customers would gather around the pot-bellied stove, not minding the smoke and the soot it gave forth.

Some of the farmers, having no cash, would bring produce to barter for their purchases. The stock of the general store was varied. There were open sacks and barrels of bulk foods like sugar, rice, coffee, and potatoes. China, soap, buttons, and cloth were bought by the women. Men often purchased tobacco, jeans, suspenders, shoes, nails, tools, guns and ammunition, and farm equipment. Many kinds of patent medicine were available and were claimed to be cures for any disease or condition.

Somewhat simpler and cleaner general stores still exist and prosper in many small towns throughout the country. They are usually family businesses, offering a wide variety of merchandise, including clothing, hardware, farm implements, groceries, and school supplies. They still serve as a place to meet and to pass along local information.

The country auction is a method of selling household goods, farm equipment, or other belongings to be disposed of because of a family's departure or a death, or for selling a collection of goods from some other source. The sale usually takes place outside the house, with the audience seated on benches, chairs, or boxes, or else standing. With the help of one or more assistants, the auctioneer displays the item offered for bidding, while praising its qualities. He has a special style of patter, speaking rapidly and dramatically. Sometimes he includes some rather gruff humor, or possibly a few insulting remarks ridiculing members of the audience who are not bidding or who are offering too little. His performance, if he is a skilled auctioneer, is quite a show; and it is not surprising that many come to watch it, with no intention of buying anything. Nevertheless, even some of those find themselves involved in bidding—perhaps for an item they do not really want. In fact, there have been cases of a person raising a hand to brush off a fly, and finding himself or herself the unwilling possessor of some strange object.

A. PRONUNCIATION

Practice differentiating [I] from [iy].

[I]	*versus*	[iy]
bid		bead
is		ease
it		eat
still		steel; steal
mitt		meat; meet
sit		seat
hit		heat
hill		heal; heel
been; bin		bean
bit		beat
lid		lead (*verb*)

B. WORD FORMATION

Adjective compounds have the same stress pattern as noun compounds: the first word in the compound receives major stress.

pot-bellied stove
hard-earned money
fresh-frozen vegetables
oil-burning heater
fast-talking auctioneer
hard-working farmer
mail-order catalogue

PRACTICE EXERCISE

Guess what each adjective compound means, and use with an appropriate noun.

Examples:

law-abiding (living according to the laws)
 a law-abiding citizen

heartfelt (deeply felt, sincere)
heartfelt sympathy

1. good-looking   4. ice-cold
2. man-made   5. snow-white
3. sunbaked   6. red-hot

C. GRAMMAR

Present tense (one-word verb) refers to an action or condition that is customary or habitual. It often appears with adverbs like *always*, *often*, *frequently*, *usually*, *never*, *hardly ever*, *rarely*, and *as a rule*.

Present progressive (with **am**, **is**, or **are** as auxiliary) refers to action going on in the immediate present (right now). It often appears with the words *right now*, *now*, *at the moment*, *at the present time*, and so on, or with information that indicates immediate present time.

PRESENT	PRESENT PROGRESSIVE
{ They bid frequently. { They never bid.	They are bidding now.
The sale usually takes place at the house.	The sale is taking place at the house right now.
They generally offer a discount.	They are offering a discount during this sale.
He always shops at Macy's.	He isn't home; he's shopping at Macy's.
I go to school by bus every day.	I am in the bus because I am going to school.
He plays tennis daily.	He is playing tennis now.

PRACTICE EXERCISE

In each blank write the correct form of the verb—either the present tense or the present progressive. After each sentence explain why you chose that tense.

Examples:

She *is talking* on the phone right now. ("*right now*")
    (talk)
They _come_ to every meeting, and they often _bring_ a friend.
   (come)   (bring)
   (*They come every time, habitually*) ("*often*" bring)

1. Jim _____ the car outside; can he call you back later?
   (wash)

2. We never _____ there; it's too far.
   (walk)

3. He _____ here now because he _____ for the bus.
   (stand)   (wait)

4. I _____ to all these concerts; I _____ them very much.
   (go)   (enjoy)

5. He always _____ in the big pool.
   (swim)

6. She can't go now; she _____ for tomorrow's exam.
   (study)

D. SPELLING

Two spellings for the sound [ɔ] are **au** and **aw**.

auction	saw
audience	law
because	raw
haul	draw
fault	straw
caution	pawn
August	hawk

E. PARAPHRASE

FORMAL	COLLOQUIAL
1. They remain.	1. They're still around.
2. They offer a wide variety of merchandise.	2. They have all kinds of {goods. {stuff.
3. serves as a place to meet.	3. is a (good) spot to meet
4. They prosper.	4. They make out fine.

F. IDIOMS

give forth = send out; produce
quite a show = an amusing performance
with no intention of _____ing = not intending to _____
find themselves involved = become involved without intending to

G. SEMANTICS

Words of related meaning:

town = urban settlement larger than a village, smaller than a city
village = small, rural settlement
hamlet = smaller than a village
crossroads = small community where roads cross, often the meeting place for people of the surrounding area

display (*verb*) = show; exhibit so that it can be seen
reveal = disclose; make known; uncover

PRACTICE EXERCISE

Fill in each blank, using one of the following words: *town, village, hamlet,* or *crossroads.*

1. After living in an apartment in the city, they settled in a peaceful _____ as farmers.

2. He was used to the quiet life of the tiny _____ where he grew up.

3. The people were proud of their _____ ; they thought it was like a city.

H. COMPREHENSION

1. Besides business, what went on in the old-time general store?
2. How did the poorer farmers pay for what they bought?
3. How does the auctioneer behave?
4. Why must visitors remember to keep their hands down?

I. SPEAKING AND WRITING

Discussion

1. Was old-time shopping more fun? How?
2. Do you suppose that there was much less shoplifting (stealing) then? Why or why not?
3. Have you ever been at an auction? Did you enjoy it?

Summary

Briefly summarize the reading selection.

26

The Rise of the Cities

Modern Chicago, which began as a trading point for western settlers. (Chicago Association of Commerce and Industry)

maintain	striking
lifeline	thrive
enlarge	deposit
expand	metropolitan
center	megalopolis
transport	continuous
junction	urban

As in other countries, the cities of the United States were usually founded where they were needed. The oldest cities grew up along the Atlantic coast, particularly where rivers flow to the ocean. These locations maintained the lifeline to Europe, which supplied both the immigrants and the imports necessary for the development of the cities. The coastal cities also kept up close contact with farms and small settlements inland along the rivers. Boston, New York, Philadelphia, Charleston, and New Orleans are among these early cities. They were greatly enlarged by the arrival of new immigrants, as well as by the growth of trade and manufacture.

As the United States expanded westward, centers developed at points where farmers' produce was collected to be transported to the cities on the coast, and where the farmers could buy manufactured goods. Such shipment sites were usually located on rivers, often where they branched (Cincinnati, Louisville, and Nashville are such sites); and later at railroad junction points, Chicago being the most striking example. These inland towns grew large as centers providing various services for the rural areas. Flour and textile mills were set up in the towns. Glass, bricks, iron, and other construction materials were manufactured there. Banks, stores, and schools were established to serve the growing population.

As manufacturing developed, cities throve near sources of power, at first near waterfalls (like Lowell, Massachusetts), then near coal and iron deposits (like Pittsburgh). Their factories attracted country people who came to find jobs. From early times restless members of farm families were drawn to the cities in search of success, but the greatest migrations from country to city took place in the last quarter of the nineteenth century and the early years of the twentieth century. It was during this period that the metropolitan centers arose, each encircled by smaller communities socially and economically dependent on it. Later the eastern megalopolis developed as a continuous urban strip from Boston through New York and Philadelphia to Washington. Not as great is the mid-western urban strip from Milwaukee, Wisconsin, to Chicago. Along the Pacific coast a megalopolis stretches from San Diego to Los Angeles, and another has developed around San Francisco.

A. PRONUNCIATION

When **t** comes after a stressed vowel and before an unstressed one, it is pronounced in ordinary American speech (not in formal or particularly precise or emphatic speech) as a flap with slight voicing—so that it sounds somewhat like an unemphatic **d** (*lettuce, water, butter, Saturday*). This flap **t** is also heard if **n** or **l** comes before the **t** (*counter, wanted, alter, melted*) and in **-tle** words (*bottle, settle, battle, little*).

city	later
Atlantic	waterfalls
settlement	greatest
center	Walter

B. WORD FORMATION

The verb prefix **en-** means 'cause to become'. Can you guess the meanings of the examples given here?

enlarge	endear
encircle	enclose
enrich	enliven
ennoble	enrage

PRACTICE EXERCISE

Fill each blank with the fitting word.

1. Her kindness and generosity _____ her to many people.

2. A metal fence _____ the whole park.

3. You can _____ the party by hiring a band to play dance music.

4. The house was too small for them; the builder _____ it by _____ the porch so that it became an extra room.

5. The child _____ the cat by pulling its tail.

C. GRAMMAR

When **which** is the object of a preposition, the preposition may either come before it or (more informally) at the end of the clause.

Europe, **from which** the necessary imports came
Europe, **which** the necessary imports came **from**

centers **to which** they could ship their produce
centers **which** they could ship their produce **to**

To which (one) was he referring?
Which (one) was he referring **to**?

PRACTICE EXERCISE

Combine each pair of sentences by using **which** instead of the underlined word(s), and use both arrangements shown above.

Examples:

They did not get the results. They had hoped for the results.
  They did not get the results for which they had hoped.
  They did not get the results which they had hoped for.

1. Chicago became a large urban center. Some country people moved to that urban center.
2. This is the book. The teacher referred to the book.
3. He opposed the plan. All the others voted for the plan.
4. That is the crime. She was accused of the crime.

D. SPELLING

A common spelling for the [ow] sound is **oa**. Here are some examples:

coast	coal
boast	loan
toast	groan
road	moan
load	foam
coat	roam
oak	approach
soak	boat

E. PARAPHRASE

FORMAL	COLLOQUIAL
1. They were greatly enlarged.	1. They got a lot bigger.
2. providing various services for the rural population	2. doing things for the country people
3. the greatest migration	3. the biggest move
4. a continuous urban strip	4. one long super-city

F. IDIOMS

took place = happened

keep up contact = communicate

where rivers branch = where streams flow into a river

G. SEMANTICS

These three words have the same pronunciation but different meanings.

sight = seeing; something seen
We saw a strange sight.

site = position or location (of a building or a settlement)
They selected a site for the new school.

cite = quote (from a book)
He always cites the Bible.

H. COMPREHENSION

1. Why are older cities often located on rivers?
2. What made the older American cities grow large?
3. Where did western towns develop?
4. Why did Chicago become a large city?
5. Why did some farm people move to the cities?
6. What was the period of greatest city growth?

I. SPEAKING AND WRITING

Discussion

1. Do you know cities outside the United States that are communication and transportation centers?
2. Why did cities grow up near sources of power?
3. How do smaller communities depend on the nearby city?
4. Do you like living (or would you like to live) in a big city? Why?

Summary

Briefly summarize the reading selection.

27

The Melting Pot

Chinese New Year parade, San Francisco—preparations for the performance of the ferocious lions. (San Francisco Convention and Visitors Bureau)

melting pot	ethnic
background	avoid
diminish	markedly
abandon	foreign
homogeneous	heritage
attain	acquaint
assimilate	reject

In its earlier years the United States was quite a successful "melting pot." The original settlers were of similar background, coming largely from northern Europe. The early immigrants continued to come chiefly from that area, and they were therefore easily absorbed. Later the western pioneers, lonely in the vast wilderness and together facing great hardships and dangers, were drawn to their neighbors of whatever origin; differences tended to diminish.

Thus developed the melting pot idea—that Americans of various backgrounds should abandon the customs and the languages of the "old country" and be absorbed into American life. People thought that the United States should serve as a melting pot and produce a homogeneous population; this was looked upon as the hope of the nation.

However, this ideal became difficult to attain in the latter part of the nineteenth century, when very large numbers of immigrants began to arrive, mainly from eastern and southern Europe. For these newcomers, assimilation was much harder because of the great differences between their cultures and languages and those of the established Americans. Feeling lost in strange surroundings, these new immigrants sought out others from their homelands, clustering together in close-knit communities. Soon many cities had ethnic neighborhoods known as "Little Italy," "Little Poland," "Chinatown," and so on.

The children of these immigrants learned American ways quickly by imitating their American schoolmates. They avoided the customs and languages of their parents and grandparents, even feeling ashamed of their non-American ways and their "broken" English. This, of course, led to unpleasant family relationships and to feelings of inferiority.

On the whole this attitude toward one's old-world background has changed markedly, especially since the middle years of this century. People of various origins have become interested in their "foreign" past and proud of their cultural heritage. Courses are organized for the study of the native language and life, which they or their parents once tried to forget. Children's books are published to acquaint the young with their ethnic past. Holidays and folk festivals of the lands of their ancestors are celebrated in public. New York's famous St. Patrick's Day parade is an example, as are the Holland bulb festival in the town of

Holland, Michigan, and the Chinese New Year's celebration in New York and in San Francisco.

Many of today's descendants of immigrants respect the cultures they had once rejected. Furthermore, they believe that the United States, a land of immigrants, would benefit by retaining aspects of its many cultural backgrounds. 35

A. PRONUNCIATION

The letter **c** before **i**, **e**, or **y** is pronounced [s]; otherwise it is pronounced [k]. Therefore, double **c** (**cc**) followed by **i**, **e**, or **y** is pronounced [ks].

succeed [sək siyd′]
successful [sək sɛs′ fəl]
accident [æk′ sə dənt]
accent [æk′ sɛnt]
access [æk′ sɛs]
accept [æk sɛpt′]

B. WORD FORMATION

Adding **-ly** to an adjective makes an adverb.

ADJECTIVE	ADVERB
large	largely
chief	chiefly
easy	easily
quick	quickly
real	really
main	mainly
marked	markedly
true	truly
sincere	sincerely
honest	honestly

A few words ending in **-ly** are themselves adjectives.

early   likely
lonely   friendly
lovely   homely

PRACTICE EXERCISE

Change these sentences so as to use the adverb instead of the adjective.

Examples:

This homework is easy to do.
   You can do this homework easily.
His statement was true.
   He spoke truly.

1. Mary's sorrow is <u>sincere</u>.
2. The student gave a <u>quick</u> answer.
3. Tom is an <u>honest</u> worker.
4. It was a <u>real</u> surprise.
5. The train was <u>slow</u>.
6. There are <u>marked</u> differences between them.
7. The <u>main</u> subject of his lecture was pollution.
8. Bill is a <u>careless</u> driver.

C. GRAMMAR

Certain verbs can be followed by an infinitive, the two having the same subject.

The immigrants *continued to come* from northern Europe.
The new immigrants *began to arrive*.
They *wished to live* near their own people.
The children *tried to forget* the old customs.
At the frontier, differences *tended to diminish*.
Later they *learned to appreciate* the culture of their ancestors.
They *are seeking to revive* the old holidays.
They *plan to celebrate* the holiday with a parade.

Notice that the verb often indicates the subject's attitude, while the infinitive names the action.

We *intend to go* to the basketball game.
We *expect to go*.
They *hope to win*.
Jim *decided to take* the job.
She *consented to come*.
Mary *volunteered to help*.

PRACTICE EXERCISE

Make up a sentence for each of the following verb-infinitive combinations.

Examples:

expect to win
    Our team *expects to win* the game.
offer to serve
    They *offered to serve* on the committee.

1. want to travel
2. refuse to pay
3. consent to go
4. threaten to quit
5. try to learn
6. promise to come
7. continue to work

D. SPELLING

Spellings for the sound [U] include **oo**, **u**, and **ou**.

1. A common spelling for [U] is **oo**.

good	took	brook
hood	look	wool
book	cook	foot

In many words, however, the spelling **oo** has a different pronunciation (see chapter 34, section D).

2. Another spelling for the sound [U] is **u**, but in many other words the pronunciation of **u** is different (see chapter 20, section A).

put
pull
full
bully

3. In these common words the [U] sound is spelled **ou**, and the **l** is silent.

should
would
could

E. PARAPHRASE

FORMAL	COLLOQUIAL
1. of whatever origin	1. no matter where they came from
2. develop into a homogeneous population	2. get to be all alike
3. feeling lost in strange surroundings	3. feeling out of things
4. learned quickly by imitating	4. caught on fast by copying
5. has changed markedly	5. has made a switch

F. IDIOMS

melting pot
= a pot in which different metals are fused (melted together)
= a merging of people so as to become alike

seek out
= make an effort in order to find

close-knit
= firmly joined together

G. SEMANTICS

evade = escape by cleverness
He used this trick to evade paying taxes.

avoid = keep away from
Her doctor told her to avoid alcohol and tobacco.

reject = refuse to accept
She applied for the job, but they rejected her.

on the whole = in general; in most ways
They made a few minor mistakes, but on the whole it was a good job.

H. COMPREHENSION

1. What made the melting-pot idea a natural one in the early days of the United States?
2. What made it less appropriate later?
3. How did "ethnic neighborhoods" develop?

4. Around 1900 how did immigrant children feel about being immigrants?
5. What is the new ethnic attitude?

I. SPEAKING AND WRITING

Discussion

1. Why did Americans like the melting-pot idea?
2. In what ways is it good for people to be different from one another?
3. Is it good for the people of a nation to be alike in anything?
4. Are there any interesting ethnic activities that go on in your area?

Summary

In a few sentences tell what you learned about the ''melting pot.''

28

Philanthropy

The ''Green Revolution''—experts of the Rockefeller Foundation showing farmers of India a new rice-growing method to produce better crops. (Rockefeller Foundation)

tradition	likewise	surplus
philanthropy	exceptional	beneficial
generosity	energetic	trustee
donate	retirement	brethren
amass	foundation	facilities
fortune (money)		

It has become an American tradition that those who attain great wealth return some of it to the public through philanthropy. An early example of this was the generosity of Amos Lawrence of Massachusetts, a wealthy merchant, who in the 1830s and afterwards contributed much money for famine relief in Ireland. He also donated generously to educational and other humanitarian causes.

In the early years of the twentieth century several men who had amassed vast fortunes likewise became great philanthropists. Andrew Carnegie, an exceptionally energetic man, who had begun working twelve hours a day when he was only fourteen years old, became one of the world's richest men by pioneering in the steel industry. After his retirement in 1900 he devoted his time and his wealth to the establishment of free public libraries. He also set up foundations for medical research and for world peace. Carnegie's belief, as he expressed it in an essay, was that the wealthy person must ''consider all surplus revenues which come to him simply as trust funds'' which he ''is strictly bound as a matter of duty to administer in the manner . . . best calculated to produce the most beneficial results for the community—the man of wealth thus becoming the mere trustee and agent for his poorer brethren.''

John D. Rockefeller, who also began as a poor boy, became fabulously rich through oil refineries and other enterprises. In his old age, in the early 1900s, he began to donate millions for beneficial undertakings. The various Rockefeller foundations support research as well as humanitarian causes in the United States and in other parts of the world. Rockefeller funds are now fighting hunger through the so-called ''green revolution,'' whereby new agricultural techniques have greatly multiplied the yield of food crops in Mexico, India, Pakistan, and parts of Africa.

Through the Ford Foundation, and based on automobile profits, Henry Ford II donated $500 million in 1950 to universities and hospitals for improving education and health. This likewise became a world-famous foundation, whose activities have spread far and wide. Some of this money was effectively spent fighting cholera and typhus in far-off Nepal.

The philanthropy of Meyer Guggenheim, who progressed from peddling to copper-mining, supports scholarship, research, and art.

Other wealthy Americans have founded universities, art museums, research institutes, and other facilities to help people and to enrich their lives.

A. PRONUNCIATION

1. In function words (grammatical words) and in some other words, **th** is pronounced voiced [ð].

the	those	thus	seethe
this	they	therefore	smooth
these	their	brother	soothe
that	them	brethren	

2. In many words **th** is pronounced voiceless [θ].

wealth	thing	thin	myth
health	think	throw	fifth
through	thought	month	sixth
philanthropy	thick	cloth	eighth

Practice making the distinction between [θ] and [ð].

bath (*noun*)	bathe (*verb*)
breath (*noun*)	breathe (*verb*)
teeth (*noun*)	teethe (*verb*)

B. WORD FORMATION

The ending **-y** is added to a noun to form an adjective.

NOUN	ADJECTIVE
wealth	wealthy
health	healthy
luck	lucky
thrift	thrifty
dirt	dirty
filth	filthy
mud	muddy
noise	noisy
shine	shiny
snow	snowy
rain	rainy
wind	windy
storm	stormy
silk	silky

PRACTICE EXERCISE

In the following sentences, change the underlined adjective to the matching noun.

Examples:

Because they were thrifty, they saved a great deal of money.
  Their thrift made it possible for them to save a great deal of money.
It was a rainy day.
  We had rain all day.

1. The cloth felt silky.
2. They stayed home because of the stormy weather.
3. His polished shoes were shiny.
4. The sled slid down the snowy hill.

C. GRAMMAR

Verb and particle combinations (see chapter 24, section C) in passive use are never split up.

ACTIVE	PASSIVE
She **set up** foundations.	Foundations **were set up**.
She **set** them **up**.	They **were set up**.
They **sought out** others from their homeland.	Others **were sought out**.
They **sought** others **out**.	Others **were sought out**.
He **thought over** the suggestion of his friend.	The suggestion **was thought over**.
He **thought** it **over**.	It **was thought over**.
She **handed down** her wealth.	Her wealth **was handed down**.
She **handed** it **down**.	It **was handed down**.
They **voted down** the amendment.	The amendment **was voted down**.
They **voted** it **down**.	It **was voted down**.
He **washed off** the ink-stain.	The ink-stain **was washed off**.
He **washed** it **off**.	It **was washed off**.
People **called out** the police.	The police **were called out**.
People **called** them **out**.	They **were called out**.

PRACTICE EXERCISE

Change these verb-particle sentences to the passive form (see chapter 16, section C and chapter 24, section C). Remember that with the passive, the **by** phrase, which names the performer of the action, is usually omitted if the subject of the matching active sentence is indefinite—*someone, people, they,* etc.

Examples:

His aunt and uncle *brought* him *up*.
   He *was brought up* by his aunt and uncle.
She *sent* the letter *out* a few days ago.
   The letter *was sent out* a few days ago.

1. They *set off* the bomb.
2. Someone *cleaned up* the apartment.
3. We *mailed* the check *in* promptly.
4. He *made* the story *up* as an excuse.
5. Jane *set* the plants *out* in the garden.
6. Someone *found* the secret *out*.
7. She *set* all the facts *down*.
8. They *turned* the water *off* in the house.

D. SPELLING

The regular spelling for the sound [č] is **ch**.

mer**ch**ant	**ch**air
charity	**ch**ampion
enri**ch**	whi**ch**
resear**ch**	

Special spellings for [č] are **tch**, **t** before a suffix beginning with *u*, and **ti** after *s* when followed by *-on* or *-an*.

ca**tch**	for**t**une	ques**ti**on
wa**tch**	pic**t**ure	diges**ti**on
ki**tch**en	na**t**ure	conges**ti**on
pi**tch**er	vir**t**uous	sugges**ti**on
sna**tch**	even**t**ually	Chris**ti**an
la**tch**	signa**t**ure	

E. PARAPHRASE

FORMAL	COLLOQUIAL
1. who had amassed vast fortunes	1. who had struck it rich
2. exceptionally energetic	2. full of pep
3. philanthropist	3. do-gooder

F. IDIOMS

far and wide = over a wide area; everywhere
here and there = in various places; scattered
to support research = to contribute money to carry on research
to enrich their lives = to make their lives more meaningful

G. SEMANTICS

Words of related meaning:

tradition = beliefs and customs handed down for many years
custom = usual way of acting
habit = tendency resulting from repeated action

H. COMPREHENSION

1. What did Carnegie believe about philanthrophy?
2. What did he support?
3. What are the Rockefeller foundations?
4. What does the Ford Foundation do?

I. SPEAKING AND WRITING

Discussion

1. Do you agree with Carnegie's opinions about wealth?
2. Why do you suppose some rich people become philanthropists?
3. What would you do if you were wealthy?

Summary

Briefly summarize the reading selection.

29

Thomas Edison, Wizard of Menlo Park

Advertisement for Edison's phonograph—the "hi-fi" instrument of 1899, powered by cranking the handle.

approach

advance (*noun*)

gratitude

solution

accept

operation

disappointment

patent

demand (*noun*)

apply

function (*verb*)

modify

device

revolutionary (*adjective*)

At the age of fifteen Thomas Edison, while selling newspapers near the railroad station, noticed a small child on the tracks as a train was approaching. He ran and pulled the child away, saving his life. In gratitude, the child's father, who was the station master, invited Edison to live in his house. He also trained him to be a telegraph operator. This work interested Edison, who had always liked to   5
experiment with mechanical devices.

A vote-counting machine that Edison invented at the age of twenty was not accepted because it was not considered useful. After that disappointment, he decided not to work on any invention until he had made sure that it would fill a demand and be accepted.   10

Inventions that greatly improved the functioning of the telegraph earned him so much money that he was able to establish a laboratory for inventions. At the age of twenty-nine he set up such an "invention factory" at Menlo Park, a New Jersey village. His team of workers included toolmakers and a physicist as well as practical designers of devices. There followed further telegraphic   15
advances, then a number of solutions for problems in the operation of Alexander Graham Bell's invention, the telephone.

In 1878 Edison invented the phonograph. The incandescent bulb was patented in 1880, when a light bulb was produced that could burn for forty hours. Electric lighting had been invented early in the century, but the practical problems   20
of lighting the streets electrically had never been worked out before. The great contribution of Edison was his applying of scientific discoveries and his modifying of older inventions so as to produce practical, usable devices. Together with his team he brought out a stream of inventions, accumulating over one thousand patents.   25

Out of Edison's work in electricity there developed the electric power and light industries and eventually a new way of living for the people of the United States and much of the rest of the world. Many other inventions from the so-called invention factory proved to be of great importance, but the remarkable work in electricity had a truly revolutionary effect on modern life.   30

A. PRONUNCIATION

1.   The letters **-ng** at the end of a word or a root are pronounced [ŋ] (see chapter 3, section A).

approaching	wrong
saving	rung
counting	along
functioning	belong
lighting	lung
accumulating	singing
living	hanging

2.   Before a suffix **-ng** is pronounced [ŋ] (as in *hanged*, *singer*), except before the comparative **-er** and the superlative **-est**. Thus, *longing* is pronounced [lɔŋiŋ]; but *longer* is [lɔŋgər], and *longest* is [lɔŋgəst].

B. WORD FORMATION

Many words in English can be used as noun or as verb without changing the form of the word.

NOUN	VERB
He took out a **patent**.	He will **patent** the invention.
The **approach** of the train is slow.	They **approach** slowly.
The machine was an **advance** over hand tools.	This will **advance** public welfare.
The **work** was completed.	They **work** hard.
There was no **demand** for it.	They **demand** practical results.
It serves a useful **function**.	It can **function** well.
He answered the **telephone**.	I often **telephone** them.
The **burn** was painful.	The lights **burn** brightly.
He improved the electric **light**.	The bulbs **light** up the room.

C. GRAMMAR

Which or **who(m)** as object of the verb (of its own clause):

Edison saved the boy. He pulled him off the track. ⟹

Edison saved the boy whom he pulled off the track.

They refused the voting machine. Edison had invented it. ⟹

They refused the voting machine, which Edison had invented.

Edison hired a team of workers. He had selected them carefully. ⟹

Edison hired a team of workers whom he had selected carefully.

Edison's team produced many inventions. He patented them. ⟹

Edison's team produced many inventions, which he patented.

PRACTICE EXERCISE

Combine each pair of sentences by using **which** (for a thing) or **who(m)** (for a person). Show by an arrow what **which** or **who** refers to.

Examples:

This is the man. I met him at the office.

This is the man whom I met at the office.

She wore the new shoes. She had bought them
    to match her dress.

She wore the new shoes, which she had bought
    to match her dress.

1. Mary finished her homework. The teacher had assigned the homework yesterday.
2. He is a new student. He comes from Brazil.
3. They fixed the fender. Jim had dented the fender in the accident.
4. We talked to the children. The children live across the street.

D. SPELLING

At the end or in the middle of a word, **ck** is a spelling for the sound [k].

track	lock	acknowledge	reckless
black	block	reckon	hockey
luck	wreck	beckon	flocking
truck			

E. PARAPHRASE

FORMAL	COLLOQUIAL
1. as a train approached the station	1. when a train was pulling in
2. to experiment with mechanical devices	2. to putter around with machinery
3. It was not accepted.	3. They didn't want it.
4. solving problems in the operation of	4. taking the kinks out of
5. a new way of living	5. a new life style

F. IDIOMS

make sure = find out with certainty; be convinced
fill a demand = supply what is desired
improved the functioning = made it work better
proved to be of great importance = was found to be important

G. SEMANTICS

Words of related meaning:

train = to make someone skilled
educate = to develop the mind and abilities by teaching

invent = devise or make up something new
discover = find or find out something which was not known before

PRACTICE EXERCISE

Fill in each blank with the fitting word from the above list.

1. Alexander Bell _____ the telephone.

2. They _____ new employees so they could use the machinery.

3. Columbus _____ America in 1492.

4. The public schools were founded in order to _____ all children, rich and poor alike.

H. COMPREHENSION

1. How did Edison become involved in telegraph work?
2. What was his first great disappointment, and what did he learn from it?
3. How did he manage to earn enough money to set up his "invention factory?"
4. What was the most important of Edison's inventions?

I. SPEAKING AND WRITING

Discussion

1. Do you think Edison would have become a great inventor even if he hadn't by chance become a telegraph operator?
2. Does the success of the "invention factory" mean that invention is a matter of carefully organized work, not of genius?
3. Would you like to live without electricity? Why or why not?
4. Why did Edison set up such a team?
5. Who do you suppose got the credit for the team's inventions?

Summary

Briefly summarize the story about Edison.

30

Jane Addams, Angel of the Slums

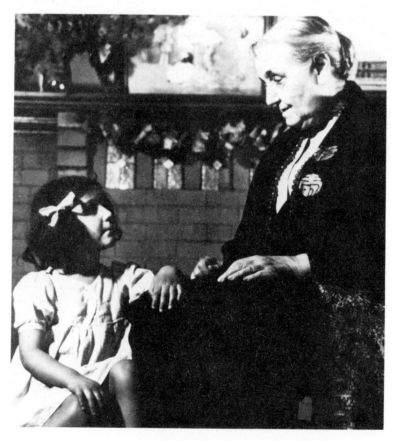

Jane Addams with one of her Hull House friends. (Chicago Historical Society)

well-to-do	situation
cultured	appreciate
distressed	disapprove
slum	meddle
initiate	promote
remarkable	responsibility
child labor	underprivileged
suffrage	contribution

Jane Addams, a member of a well-to-do, cultured family, was so distressed about the misery of the poor that she left home to spend her life in the slums of Chicago. In 1889 she established a "settlement house" there, called Hull House, where she initiated many humanitarian projects. Among these were hot-lunch service for factory workers, day-care centers for little children, free [5] classes for young people and for adults, a gymnasium, and an art gallery. Immigrants and other poor people came to Jane Addams's Hull House to get advice and help, as well as to learn and to have fun. This remarkable woman also devoted herself to a number of other causes. She was active in fighting against the use of child labor and against war; she worked for woman's suffrage and for improving [10] the situation of the blacks; and she helped to establish playgrounds and public parks and initiated country vacation programs for poor city children.

Not everyone appreciated the work of Jane Addams. Indeed some disapproved of what they considered her meddling in other people's affairs. Nevertheless, she exerted great influence on the development of social work in the [15] United States and also in other parts of the world. She promoted the idea of responsibility for the welfare of the underprivileged, and her programs were widely adopted. Settlement houses modeled on Hull House were founded in many poor neighborhoods to help children and adults to make their lives more meaningful. [20]

In recognition of her contributions to society, Jane Addams was awarded the Nobel peace prize in 1931.

A. PRONUNCIATION

Between vowels, or at the end of a word after a vowel, **s** is usually pronounced [z]. (Exceptions like *measure*, *usual*, *vision* will be dealt with in chapter 35, section D2.)

misery	causes	was	rises
these	houses	has	closes
nose	phrases	knows	
boys	is	goes	

B. WORD FORMATION

The adjective endings **-able** and **-ible** are pronounced [əbəl]. The stress falls on the immediately preceding syllable.

a remarkable woman
a terrible accident
a lovable child
a responsible person
unbreakable toys
digestible food
washable fabrics
a curable disease

PRACTICE EXERCISE

Match each adjective with the appropriate noun on the right.

ADJECTIVE	NOUN
wearable	bed
believable	clothing
changeable	worker
comfortable	business
profitable	coat
unbreakable	story
dependable	accident
avoidable	glass
fashionable	weather

C. GRAMMAR

Verbs of transfer (*give, tell, sell, buy, ask, offer, pay, lend, show, hand*) take two objects. The first is the indirect object, referring to the one to whom or for whom the action is done, and the second is the direct object of the verb.

INDIRECT   DIRECT
OBJECT   OBJECT

She gave the workers hot lunches.
  (She gave hot lunches to the workers.)

INDIRECT OBJECT   DIRECT OBJECT

They awarded Jane Addams the Nobel prize.
  (They awarded the Nobel prize to Jane Addams.)

INDIRECT   DIRECT

He told the people the truth.
  (He told the truth to the people.)

PRACTICE EXERCISE

Change each sentence by replacing the prepositional phrase with an indirect object. Label the direct object and the indirect object.

Examples:

INDIRECT   DIRECT

We bought Mary a gift.
  (We bought a gift for Mary.)

INDIRECT   DIRECT

She handed me the book.
  (She handed the book to me.)

1. Mary sold the textbook to her roommate.
2. The teacher told an interesting story to the children.
3. Ted showed the book to his friends.
4. They offered the job to Amy.
5. We sent a letter to them.
6. Tom's father lent the car to him.
7. She gave a ten-dollar bill to the cashier.
8. The visitor brought toys for the children.

D. SPELLING

Words for special spelling practice:

    gymnasium
    fight
    people
    neighbor
    special
    encourage
    trouble

E. PARAPHRASE

FORMAL	COLLOQUIAL
1. She was distressed about the misery of the poor.	1. She was upset about the troubles poor people.
2. She initiated many humanitarian programs.	2. She got a lot of welfare projects going.
3. improving their situation	3. getting them a better deal
4. exerted great influence	4. made a big dent
5. Not everyone appreciated her work.	5. Some people took a dim view of work.

F. IDIOMS

well-to-do; well off = prosperous; rich
promote (the idea) = foster; encourage
modeled on = imitating
take a dim view of = disapprove of

G. SEMANTICS

Some words of similar meaning:

initiate = begin; get something started
establish = set up on a firm basis
found = set up for the present and for the future

H. COMPREHENSION

1. What is a settlement house?
2. What were the "causes" of Jane Addams?
3. What principle did Jane Addams make people aware of?
4. How did people imitate her work?

I. SPEAKING AND WRITING

Discussion

1. Many kind people become depressed or angry about the condition of the underprivileged. How was Jane Addams different from such people?

2. What was similar in all the causes that Jane Addams was active in?
3. What do you suppose Jane Addams's critics thought about her?

Summary

Briefly summarize what you learned about Jane Addams.

31

The Chicanos

Chicanos celebrating a fiesta. (Denver Public Library)

employer	typical
scout (*noun*)	barrier
disturbance	bilingual
housing	comprehend
barrio	maintain

The big migration of Mexicans into the southwestern states of the United States began about 1900. At that time a great increase in railroad building and in agriculture led to a need for more workers. Some employers actually sent scouts across the border to recruit Mexican laborers. In times of unemployment and of political disturbances in their homeland, more Mexicans crossed over to the 5 United States. Some of them came for the summer season, when there was a great deal of farm work; others moved in to stay. The whole family would work in gathering the crops, and they would move from farm to farm as their labor was needed.

Where the migrant workers' housing has been set up by the farm owner, it 10 is often very poor. But in some places workers' camps have been built with government help, and there the situation is better. In these camps there are small individual houses with electricity and other conveniences. Some of these communities include child-care centers, where small children are cared for while their parents are at work. 15

Many Mexican-Americans are employed in factories. Some of the largest communities of Chicanos (Mexican-Americans) are in Los Angeles and other California cities, in Denver, and in Chicago. The larger *barrios* (Chicano neighborhoods) have stores where Mexican foods, toys, and other typical goods are sold. On September 16, Mexican Independence Day, there are lively celebrations 20 in these communities, especially in San José, California. On that occasion many of the people dress in Mexican costumes and sing, dance, and have fun. Thus the Chicanos bring some pleasure into their hard life.

One of the problems that have made it difficult for Chicanos to succeed in the United States is the language barrier. The migrants speak Spanish, and their 25 children grow up with Spanish as their native language. In school many of them have great difficulty understanding and learning because instruction there is in English. Therefore a large number of them become discouraged and leave school. To cope with this problem some of the cities with a large Chicano population have set up bilingual school systems in Spanish-speaking neighborhoods. During the 30 early school years the children are taught the basic subjects (such as arithmetic and history) in their native language, so that they can comprehend the new ideas.

Meanwhile they are taught English by various methods, often with the help of modern learning devices. At a certain stage in their schooling they are ready to join other American pupils in regular school classes conducted in English, while Spanish is maintained as a language and literature subject for them. This kind of education is valuable in preventing failure in school and "dropping out," and also in bolstering the student's sense of pride in his or her cultural background.

In recent years some Mexican-Americans have been working to improve the situation of their people. Cesar Chavez was particularly well-known for his leadership of the farm workers in his tireless efforts to better their working conditions and their wages. Many Mexican-Americans have succeeded in entering various professional fields such as teaching and law. A number of Mexican-Americans have even been elected to Congress or have been chosen to fill high government positions.

A. PRONUNCIATION

Practice closing the lips to say [m].

employment	costume
time	problem
family	system
migration	method
community	modern
September	comprehend

B. WORD FORMATION

Here is an example of a basic word with its suffixes and a prefix.

employ	
employer	
employee (one who works for an employer)	
employed	unemployed
employment	unemployment
employable	unemployable

Can you guess the meanings of *employable* and *unemployable*?

C. GRAMMAR

Adverb clauses beginning with **when** indicate time. Adverb clauses beginning with **where** indicate place.

when there was farm work
when the parents are at work
when there was great unemployment
where the housing was set up by the farmer
where Mexican foods are sold
where they dress in Mexican costumes

PRACTICE EXERCISE

Complete the following sentences by adding an independent clause to the **when** or **where** clause. (Remember that a clause contains a subject and its verb.)

Examples:

When there was farm work in the United States, *some Mexican laborers crossed over the border.*
Some Chicano children go to schools where they learn English.

1. When Mexican immigrants celebrate Mexican Independence Day, ___ .

2. Where many Mexicans live close together, _____ .

3. When there is great unemployment in Mexico, _____ .

4. _____ where they study along with American children.

5. When children become discouraged at school, _____ .

6. When I was a child, _____ .

7. _____ where the road makes a sharp turn.

D. SPELLING

Write the apostrophe *after* the s of a plural noun to indicate possession.

    workers' camps = camps of workers
    employers' scouts = scouts for employers
    Chicanos' problems = problems of Chicanos
    pupils' classes = classes of pupils

Write the apostrophe *before* the **s** when the possessor is singular.

>   a worker's job = the job of a worker
>   an employer's factory = the factory of an employer
>   this man's wife = the wife of this man
>   that pupil's book = the book of that pupil

PRACTICE EXERCISE

Reword each phrase, using the possessive noun form.

Examples:

>   the owner of that dog—that dog's owner
>   shoes for boys—boys' shoes

1. the house of the migrant
2. houses of migrants
3. communities of Chicanos
4. the name of this teacher
5. the language of that student
6. dolls for little girls
7. the books of the students
8. the mother of that boy
9. the problems of a foreigner
10. the problems of foreigners

E. PARAPHRASE

FORMAL	COLLOQUIAL
1. {their native language / their mother tongue	1. {the language they were born to / their first language
2. became successful	2. {came up in the world / did all right / made it / made good
3. There are lively celebrations.	3. They have a {great / hot} time.
4. to improve the situation	4. to make things better

F. IDIOMS

a great deal of = much; lots of
the language barrier = the problem of not knowing the language
dropping out = leaving school or some other responsibility
as needed = when and where it is needed

G. SEMANTICS

Words of related meaning:

job = employment, temporary or regular, usually at work that is not of high status
position = regular employment at work that is more highly respected than an ordinary job
wages = payment for a job, usually by the day or the week, sometimes for a longer period
salary = payment for a regular position, usually by the month or the year

H. COMPREHENSION

1. What conditions encouraged Mexicans to come to the United States at the beginning of this century?
2. Why are these farm workers called migrants?
3. In which part of the country do most of the Chicanos live?
4. What happens on Mexican Independence Day?
5. Why are the little children taught arithmetic in Spanish?
6. Who is Cesar Chavez?

I. SPEAKING AND WRITING

Discussion

1. Would you like to spend a summer picking crops in California? In what ways would it be an interesting experience?
2. How would life in the barrio be different from that in other communities?

3. How do you think the Chicano parents feel about continuing their children's study of Spanish in school? Why?
4. What would you expect the farm owners' attitude to be toward Chavez?

Summary

Briefly tell what you learned about Mexican-Americans.

32

Farming Today

Harvesting rice—modern farming with expensive and powerful machines. (Courtesy of the Rice Council)

swell (*verb*)	progress
ally (*noun*)	available
cultivation	boon
process	characteristic (*adjective*)
perform	enterprise

The early 1900s was a time of exceptional city growth. This greatly increased the demand for food from the farms. In fact, the price of farm produce grew threefold in the first two decades of the century. World War I swelled the demand for food, since the United States was helping to feed its overseas allies. During the war farmers put more land under cultivation and bought trucks and machinery, including power pumps and power saws. McCormick reapers were particularly in demand on the farms of the western plains. Machines for plowing, seeding, binding, and other farm work were widely adopted. As one process was speeded up, there arose a need to perform the others faster, and therefore to buy additional machinery.

Scientific agriculture also developed in this period. With the help and guidance of the United States Department of Agriculture and of state agricultural colleges, farmers began to take advantage of scientific progress in soil-testing, fertilizing with chemicals, and the testing and treatment of animals and plants for diseases. Efficient methods became available for killing harmful insects and weeds, and botanical experimentation led to the development of improved varieties of vegetables and grains.

The Rural Electrification Act of 1936 was a great boon to farmers. In 1935 only ten percent of the nation's farms had electricity, but the power lines that were established as a result of this law brought electricity within the reach of almost all farmers. Farm life has also become much more convenient and pleasant because of the automobile and the telephone. There are now more opportunities for social contact. The children of farmers now travel by bus to modern, excellently equipped consolidated schools that serve a large area.

On the other hand, the single-family farm, once characteristic of United States agriculture, is becoming a thing of the past. The high cost of modern machinery and the growing world demand for food have led to large-scale farming. It has become necessary—and profitable—to operate huge farms and to manage them as big business enterprises. Many individual farmers have not been able to compete, and have had to give up farming. Consequently only 2.2 percent of the population now live on farms, and those who still do are no longer self-sufficient.

A. PRONUNCIATION

In practicing long words, remember to keep unstressed syllables very short.

ex**cep**tional	**prof**itable
situ**a**tion	**con**sequently
culti**va**tion	elec**tri**city
ma**chin**ery	con**sol**idated
par**tic**ularly	**en**terprises
ad**di**tional	characte**ris**tic
agriculture	indi**vid**ual
ef**fi**cient	popu**la**tion
suf**fi**cient	**bus**iness [bIz, nIs]

B. WORD FORMATION

The noun endings **-ance** and **-ence** are used in abstract nouns (idea nouns) based on verbs or on **-ant** and **-ent** adjectives.

VERB	NOUN
appear	appearance
assist	assistance
guide	guidance

ADJECTIVE	NOUN
important	importance
brilliant	brilliance
different	difference
excellent	excellence
independent	independence

C. GRAMMAR

1. Prepositional phrases or adverbs of time and of place. A prepositional phrase indicating place usually comes after the verb (and its object if there is one) or possibly at the beginning of the sentence. A time-phrase may come in either of these positions. When prepositional phrases or adverbs of time and of place are used together, the place-phrase or adverb usually comes right after the verb (and its object), and the time-phrase comes last.

```
          PLACE         TIME
         ‿‿‿‿‿‿      ‿‿‿‿‿
He arrived at the house after midnight
```

```
                                    PLACE            TIME
                                 ‿‿‿‿‿‿‿‿‿‿       ‿‿‿‿‿‿
Scientific agriculture developed in the United States at that time.
```

PRACTICE EXERCISE

Place the time and the place modifiers after the verb in the usual order.

Example:

The power lines brought electricity (in a short while; to the farms).
   The power lines brought electricity to the farms in a short while.

1. She came (here; at ten o'clock).
2. We'll be (soon; there).
3. Your order will be delivered (there; by nine o'clock).
4. She returned (recently; home).
5. They traveled (last year; north).
6. He comes (after school; here).

2.   Prepositional phrases beginning with **in**, **within**, **at**, and some other prepositions usually have to do with place (that is, location and space).

PLACE

in deals with the place in general:
   in the house

within means 'inside the limits of a place':
   within the area
   within the boundaries of the state

at gives the location exactly:
   at the street corner

but these prepositions are also used with reference to time.

TIME

in places the action with respect to time:
   in 1935
   in the first two decades
   in this period

within means 'in the course of' or 'inside the limits of the time':
> He completed it within one week (between the beginning and the
> end of the week).
> There were three earthquakes within a decade.

at points to an exact time:
> at noon
> at half past ten
> at the time of his death
> At the signal, they all began to run.

D. SPELLING

i-_consonant_**-e** is the regular spelling for the sound [ay], often called "long *i*."

time	white
price	while
fertilize	ride
enterprise	dime
line	like
life	hike

i-_consonant_**-e** is a special spelling for the sound [iy].

automobile
machine
gasoline
marine
ravine

E. PARAPHRASE

FORMAL	COLLOQUIAL
1. It was a time of exceptional growth for the city.	1. The city grew {very / awfully} fast then.
2. It was a great boon.	2. It was a big help.
3. The power lines brought electricity within the reach of all farmers.	3. All farmers could get electricity.

F. IDIOMS

take advantage of = make use of; profit by
on the other hand = in contrast; however
becoming a thing of the past = disappearing
under cultivation = being worked on for growing crops

G. SEMANTICS

Here are three words that are quite similar in meaning:

self-sufficient = able to supply one's needs unaided
The farmer who grew enough food for his family, cut down trees for building and for fuel, and used wool from his sheep for clothing was self-sufficient.

independent = not relying on others; thinking and acting on one's own
Their daughter wants to leave school and get a job in order to become independent.
The independent voter decides for himself or herself, not just following the line of his or her party or the opinions of other people.

self-reliant = seeking no help from others; having faith in oneself
The pioneer was proud of being self-reliant.

PRACTICE EXERCISE

Write the appropriate word in each blank.

1. He did not want any money from his parents; he wanted to prove that he was _____.

2. Unlike the old-time farmer, today's farmer is not really _____.

3. Young people are often eager to become _____, even when they are not yet mature enough to manage their lives.

4. This candidate has been appealing to the _____ voter, who thinks for herself/himself.

H. COMPREHENSION

1. What increased the demand for farm products?
2. Which kinds of farm machinery were adopted by the farmers?
3. How did advances in science help the farmers?
4. What did the Rural Electrification Act do for them?
5. What changes took place in the size and the management of American farms?

I. SPEAKING AND WRITING

Discussion

1. Do you think that a system of small, one-family farms is better for the farmers, or for the nation? Why?
2. How is a family's life changed by having electricity?
3. How is a farm family's life changed by having farm machinery?

Summary

Briefly summarize what you have learned about farming in the United States.

33

Modern American Architecture

Exterior view of the Guggenheim Museum, one of the famous buildings of Frank Lloyd Wright. (Robert E. Mates)

architecture	unique
erect	worsen
plate glass	congestion
resemble	creative
canyon	blend

For better or for worse, the skyscraper is America's gift to architecture. This kind of construction became possible when light but strong steel frames could be erected and after powerful elevators had been developed. Concrete and plate glass also play an important part in building such tall structures.

Louis Sullivan, the pioneer architect of skyscrapers, built the first one in Chicago in 1884. Before long New York began constructing them, and soon every large city—as well as every city that wished to be considered important—followed suit. As the number of its skyscrapers increased, some of New York's central streets began to resemble canyons between high walls. Therefore a city law was passed, ruling that the upper stories of tall buildings must be set back so that some light and air could come through to the street. As a result, New York has a unique as well as a very interesting skyline.

Although skyscrapers are built upward because of crowding in the city and the need for additional working and living space, they have actually worsened the congestion, since they draw large numbers of people into small areas.

Modern architecture in the United States has produced other creative styles. Perhaps the most famous is the work of Frank Lloyd Wright in the first half of this century. Wright designed many original public buildings and homes, using interesting, unusual materials and trying to make each structure blend into its surroundings. His ideas have greatly influenced the architects of today.

A. PRONUNCIATION

Include all the consonants in pronouncing a consonant cluster.

split	in**fl**uen**ced**
street	**ar**chite**cts**
glass	wan**ts**
con**str**uction	chang**ed**
skyscrapers	con**gest**ion [kən jɛs' čən]
structures	**ar**chitecture [ar' kI tɛk čər]
in**t**eresting	

B. WORD FORMATION

Adding **-en**, a causative ending, to some adjectives forms causative verbs. For example, adding **-en** to **worse** forms the verb **worsen**, which means 'cause to become worse' or 'make worse', (or 'become worse').

ADJECTIVE	CAUSATIVE VERB
dark	darken
loose	loosen
hard	harden
soft	soften
sweet	sweeten
long	lengthen
strong	strengthen

C. GRAMMAR

Causative meaning can be expressed (1) by a causative verb, or (2) by its corresponding adjective following *get*, *become*, or *make*.

It *worsened* the congestion. The congestion *got worse*.

The exercises *strengthened* his muscles. The exercises made his muscles *strong*. His muscles *became strong* by exercise.

This *loosened* the knot. This *made* the knot *loose*. The knot *became loose*.

PRACTICE EXERCISE

Change the following sentences, using *get*, *become*, or *make* with an adjective instead of the causative (-**en**) verb. (In forming the causative, *get* and *become* have the same meaning, but *become* is more formal or literary.)

Example:

As the mixture dries, it *hardens*.
As the mixture dries, it *gets hard*.

1. After the sun set, the sky darkened.
2. The added sugar sweetened the dessert.
3. She turned the volume down, to soften the sound.
4. In the late afternoon, shadows lengthen.

5. The fruit ripens in September.
6. They were repaving the street in order to widen it.

D. SPELLING

qu for [kw]		**cqu** for [kw]	**qu** for [k]
quality	quote	acquire	unique
question	equip	acquaintance	antique
quarrel	inquire	acquit	liquor
quarter	request		conquer
quick	conquest		
quiet			

E. PARAPHRASE

FORMAL	COLLOQUIAL
1. This kind of construction became possible.	1. They were able to build like this.
2. The streets began to resemble canyons.	2. The streets got to look like canyons.
3. Wright designed many original buildings.	3. Wright drew up many new building plans.
4. wished to be considered important	4. wanted to { be big league / be big time / look big }

F. IDIOMS

play a part (in) = contribute; help; participate
for better or for worse = whether it is desirable or not; whether you like it
or not
follow suit = imitate; copy after
on hand = available

G. SEMANTICS

pioneer (*noun*) = first, and leader of a new trend
Newton was a pioneer in physics.

unique (*adjective*) = the only one of its kind; having no equal
  The work of a real artist is unique.
original (*adjective*) = independently thought out; novel
  Is this the original statue, or a copy?
creative (*adjective*) = productive in an original way
  She is a creative painter.

H. COMPREHENSION

1. What had to be available in order to make skyscraper building possible?
2. How did the skyscraper fashion begin?
3. Why are the upper stories of New York's high buildings set back?
4. What is the effect of skycrapers on the crowding in the city? Why?

I. SPEAKING AND WRITING

Discussion

1. Do you agree with Frank Lloyd Wright's ideas about houses and buildings?
2. Is it true that inventions and new methods appear after certain materials and equipment have been developed? Do you know why Leonardo da Vinci's "flying machine" could not fly?

Summary

Briefly summarize the reading selection.

34

The City

City Center, Philadelphia. (Philadelphia Redevelopment Authority)

core	occupant
quarters	expose
modest	progressive
limit	troubled
deteriorated	deplorable
drifter	concerted

The typical American city has as its center the business district, which includes public buildings, banks, department stores, tall office buildings, hotels, and often some elegant apartment houses. Surrounding this core there is usually an area of poorer, less attractive business establishments and a variety of crowded living quarters. Farther out are modest row houses inhabited by ''blue-collar'' 5 workers and their families. Towards the outer limits of the city are the more comfortable and attractive residential areas, with private houses and apartment buildings, often surrounded with lawns and trees.

A crowded, deteriorated part of the city is called a slum. Here the lowest-income population lives, including newcomers to the United States who have not 10 yet established themselves economically. Poor rural people coming to the city to look for work move into the slums, adding to the crowding, and there are also homeless drifters there. Slum houses are apt to be old and badly neglected by their owners as well as by their occupants. Children growing up in such neighborhoods have no fit place to play and are constantly exposed to disease and to bad 15 influences.

Ever since the late years of the past century progressive thinkers and leaders have been troubled about the deplorable conditions of the slums and have aroused the attention of the general public to this problem. As a result there arose a concerted attempt to improve the housing and the general environment of the 20 slum-dwellers. This has proved a long and difficult task. Despite the earnest efforts of various private groups as well as government agencies, many of the problems have not yet been solved, and much remains to be done.

A. PRONUNCIATION

The [yuw] sound is represented by the spelling **u** and sometimes by **iew**.

unite(d)	pop**u**lation	f**u**el
usual	c**u**te	m**u**seum
university	ac**u**te	occ**u**pant
use	exc**u**se	re**view**
uranium	ref**u**se	**view**

But the letter **u** is pronounced [ʌ] in the prefixes **un-** (*unseen*) and **under-** (*undertake*), and generally in closed syllables (*but, lump, button, Sunday*).

B. WORD FORMATION

Past participles of verbs are often used as adjectives. (The past participle is the form of the verb used after **have**.)

> *crowded* neighborhoods
> *deteriorated* houses
> *neglected* children
> *exposed* places
> *improved* conditions
> *lost* child
> *painted* walls
> *broken* windows
> *ruined* buildings

PRACTICE EXERCISE

Use the following past participles as adjectives, with an appropriate noun after each. (Look up the meaning of any participle that you are not familiar with.)

1. improved
2. furnished
3. rebuilt
4. torn
5. littered
6. polluted
7. damaged
8. renovated
9. restored
10. painted

C. GRAMMAR

In written English and in formal spoken style a sentence may begin with a place-expression followed by a verb of being, with the subject of the sentence after it. Sometimes the "empty" **there** comes after the place-expression.

> Farther out are modest row houses.
> Toward the outer limits of the city are the more attractive houses.

Surrounding this core there is usually a poor neighborhood.
Beyond the city limits there may be a ring of suburbs.

PRACTICE EXERCISE

Write the four sentences listed in section C, underlining each subject with a single line, and its verb with a double line.

D. SPELLING

The sound [uw] has several spellings.

oo	u-*consonant*-e	ew	ue	ough
boot	tune	grew	true	through
too	prune	blew	blue	
moon	student	flew	clue	
soon	tube	knew	sue	
room	rude	new	due	

E. PARAPHRASE

FORMAL	COLLOQUIAL
1. This has proved a long and difficult task.	1. This has been a tough job.
2. a concerted attempt to improve it	2. a drive to make it better
3. inhabited by working people	3. where working people live
4. establish themselves economically	4. { get to be well off / become prosperous
5. constantly exposed to disease	5. always liable to catch (come down with) something

F. IDIOMS

such as = like
call (it) to their attention = show them
as a result = consequently; therefore

G. SEMANTICS

These three past participles used as adjectives often describe the slums:

deteriorated = in bad condition
decayed = rotted; falling apart
dilapidated = neglected; broken down

H. COMPREHENSION

1. What is to be found around the central business district?
2. What are the living conditions there?
3. Has anything been done about them?
4. Where are the most pleasant residential neighborhoods?

I. SPEAKING AND WRITING

Discussion

1. If you lived in a good residential part of the city, would you be interested in the problems of the slums? Why, or why not?
2. If groups of interested citizens as well as government agencies have been working on improving the conditions of the deteriorated neighborhoods, why have they not solved the problem?

Summary

Briefly summarize what you learned about the arrangement of the American city.

35

The Automobile
in American Life

Crowded automobile traffic in New York City. (Ken Karp)

role	boon
integral	relieve
convenient	isolation
transportation	violate
foster	responsible
contribute	peer
leisure	status

The private automobile has long played an important role in the United States. In fact, it has become an integral part of the American way of life. In 1986 sixty-nine percent of American families owned at least one car, and thirty-eight percent had more than one. By giving workers rapid, convenient transportation, the automobile has freed them from having to live near their place of work. This has fostered the growth of the suburbs, but it has also led to traffic problems in the city. In addition, the automobile has contributed to the weakening of neighborhood ties by making it easy to keep up friendships at a distance and to enjoy leisure activities far from home.

For farm families the automobile is a great boon. It has relieved their isolation, making it possible for them to travel to town frequently for business and for pleasure, and also to transport their children to distant schools.

Family life has been affected in various ways. The car helps to keep families together when it is used for picnics, outings, camping trips, and other shared experiences. However, when teen-age children have the use of the car (or own one), they can easily escape from family supervision. If they are immature, they sometimes become involved in situations that lead to serious trouble. There is even greater danger if the driver (young or old) has been drinking alcohol or taking drugs—or is "showing off" by speeding or violating other traffic laws. Mothers of victims of such accidents have formed an organization called MADD (Mothers Against Drunk Driving). These women want to prevent further tragedies. They have worked to encourage the government to establish and enforce a national minimum drinking age. They send speakers to schools and to meetings of citizens to impress people with the importance of careful, responsible driving. Students have formed a similar organization (SADD, Students Against Drunk Driving) and are spreading the same message among their peers.

For many Americans the automobile is a necessity as well as a convenience. But for some, it is also a mark of social status, an important middle-class symbol; and for young people, a sign of becoming an adult. Altogether, cars mean very much to Americans.

A. PRONUNCIATION

Final **-y** is usually pronounced [i].

twenty	petty	early
family	necessity	party
city	very	carry
frequently	lovely	marry
easily	pity	ferry
opportunity	sorry	lately

B. WORD FORMATION

The prefix **re-** (often meaning 'again', 'back') appears in many verbs.

renew	repay
rebuild	repeat
refresh	reply
restore	regain
repair	return

PRACTICE EXERCISE

Guess the meanings of the following verbs, and use the verbs to complete the sentences.

Examples:

After the fire they <u>rebuilt</u> the house.
I hope that this success will help him to <u>regain</u> his self-confidence.

retrain	refill
repave	rearrange
renew	review
reappear	remarry

1. The sun, which had been hidden by clouds, _____.

2. Since there are no jobs available in their specialty, they must be _____ in order to find other kinds of work.

3. The city must _____ this street to make it smooth.

4. She decided to _____ the furniture to make the room more attractive.

5. He wants to _____ his notes before the exam.

6. A year after her husband died, she _____.

7. They _____ the empty jar with water.

8. The period of treatment and rest _____ his health.

C. GRAMMAR

Adverbs of frequency (*always*, *never*, *sometimes*, *often*, *rarely*) come before a one-word verb (other then *be*) or before the second word of the verb.

> The automobile has **long** played a role in our lives.
> It is **often** used by farm families.
> Young drivers **sometimes** become involved.
> Cars have **always** meant much to Americans.
> Does he **often** use his car?
> Their car has **never** been repaired at this auto shop.

PRACTICE EXERCISE

Put the adverb in the correct place.

Examples:

He comes to class on time. (rarely)
    He *rarely* comes to class on time.
They have regretted that decision. (often)
    They have *often* regretted that decision.

1. We have traveled by helicopter. (never)
2. Does Mary finish her homework? (ever)
3. Bill drives to school. (often)
4. They swim in the pool. (sometimes)
5. We play tennis together. (always)
6. She can find her keys. (never)
7. Tom complains about his job. (frequently)
8. I have seen such a beautiful view. (rarely)

D. SPELLING

1. When a suffix is added to a word ending in **y** after a consonant, the **y** is changed to **i**. If the suffix begins with **i**, the **y** remains.

pity	pitiful	pitying
	pitiless	
copy	copied	copying
lovely	loveliest	
	loveliness	
lonely	lonelier	
	loneliness	
easy	easily	
	easiest	
beauty	beautiful	
baby		babyish
lobby		lobbyist

2. The sound [ž] is rather rare in English. It comes only at the end of a word, where it is spelled **ge**, or within a word before **ion** or before **u**, where it is spelled **s**. (In a few cases before **u** it is spelled **z**.) The sound [ž] is the voiced form of [š].

s	s	z	ge
decision	usual	seizure	rouge
conclusion	visual	azure	beige
vision	measure		corsage
confusion	pleasure		barrage
collision	treasure		
occasion	leisure		

E. PARAPHRASE

FORMAL	COLLOQUIAL
1. has become an integral part	1. has become part and parcel (of)
2. contributes to weakening neighborhood ties	2. tends to break up the neighborhood
3. They can escape from family supervision.	3. Their parents can't keep an eye on them.
4. a mark of social status	4. {something to show off with / something to give him (her) class.

F. IDIOMS

> play a role (in) = have a part (in); have influence (in)
> to some extent = somewhat
> speed limit = fastest legal speed
> show off = display boastfully

G. SEMANTICS

Words of related meaning:

> **immature** = not developed; not yet developed; childish
> **young** = in the early years of life
> **juvenile** = a young person

H. COMPREHENSION

1. How has the automobile helped to develop the suburbs?
2. How do farm families use their cars?
3. What troubles and dangers can cars lead to?
4. What do some people want cars for, besides their practical uses?
5. What is MADD, and what does it do?

I. SPEAKING AND WRITING

Discussion

1. Do you think Americans have too many cars? Why?
2. If you were the parent of a teenage driver, would you buy him or her a car? Why, or why not?

Summary

Briefly tell what you have learned about Americans and their cars.

36

Suburbia

The Bergen Mall, Paramus, N.J., a typical suburban shopping center.

greenery	proximity
outlying	ample
decentralization	political
traffic artery	essential
resident	corruption
dwell	facility

As the cities became more crowded and as the means of transportation improved, middle-class residents of the city began to move out beyond its borders. In the suburbs they could find safer, more attractive places to live, with open space and greenery around them; yet they could travel daily to the city for their work or business. They could also attend cultural events or gatherings in the city. Soon the outlying farmlands and woods around cities turned into residential neighborhoods. Schools were established, and various types of business were developed to serve the needs of the suburban population.

During the past three or four decades there has been further decentralization of retail business as shopping malls have been built in the suburbs. These large centers, located on main traffic arteries, include mainly supermarkets, clothing stores, restaurants, and sometimes movie theaters. Their great attraction for suburban dwellers is not only proximity but also ample parking space. The chief problems of city shopping are thus avoided.

Politically the suburbs have been independent units, each with its own local government running the schools, the police and firefighting organizations, and other essential services. This arrangement has both advantages and disadvantages. Because the political units are small and the populations quite homogeneous, political corruption has almost always been avoided, and services have usually been excellent. But from the point of view of the city dwellers it is quite unfair, since it allows suburbanites to use the city's facilities and services without carrying a share of the city's tax burden or having to be concerned with the city's economic or political problems.

A. PRONUNCIATION

The sound [ɔ] contrasts with [ow], which has a glide.

[ɔ]	versus	[ow]
law		low
raw		row
saw		so; sew

call	coal
hall	hole
ball	bowl
nought	note
bought	boat
lawn	loan
jaw	Joe
flaw	flow
almost	**lo**cal
small	both
dawn	**own**
store	**only**
more	**open**
four	load
broad	rode; road
awful	**o**val

B. WORD FORMATION

-al is an adjective ending. Many adjectives ending in **-al** are based on related nouns.

NOUN	ADJECTIVE
center	central
culture	cultural
residence	residential
politics	political
essence	essential
accident	accidental
	local
	rural

C. GRAMMAR

The verb **become** is followed by a noun or an adjective that refers to the subject of **become** (compare with chapter 21, section C).

The farmlands have become residential neighborhoods.

The suburbs became political units.

The shopping malls will become business centers.

The cities became crowded.

The city's tax burden has become heavy.

The suburbs became independent.

PRACTICE EXERCISE

Complete the following sentences with an adjective or noun and point an arrow from that word to the subject that it refers to.

Example:

After so many years of experience, he became skillful in this procedure.

1. Since the accident, people have become _____.

2. The children became _____ at the sudden noise.

3. When he won the literature prize, the author became _____.

4. The city became even more _____ after so many skyscrapers were built.

5. We hope that all our students will become _____.

6. Many people can't buy a house because prices have become _____.

7. By jogging every day, John hopes that he will become _____.

8. When she graduates from medical school, she will become a _____.

9. After the heavy rain the ground became _____.

D. SPELLING

Before double **l** or **l** plus another consonant, **a** is usually pronounced [ɔ].

all	mall	recall	halt
tall	call	install	salt
ball	small	appall	bald
wall	stall	befall	falter
fall			always

E. PARAPHRASE

FORMAL	COLLOQUIAL
1. The population was quite homogeneous.	1. They were people of the same kind.
2. There has been further decentralization of retail business.	2. More stores have moved out of the center.
3. They attracted the suburban population.	3. They made a hit with the people of the suburbs.
4. The chief problem was thus avoided.	4. That's how they got rid of the main trouble.
5. without carrying their share of the burden	5. not pulling their weight

F. IDIOMS

from their point of view = as it affects them; as they see it
serve the needs = meet the requirements; provide what is necessary
traffic arteries = highways
running the schools = managing the schools
carrying one's share of the burden = doing one's part; helping proportionately

G. SEMANTICS

The words in the right-hand column mean the opposite of the words in the left-hand column.

homogeneous   **heterogeneous**
= of the same kind

advantage   **disadvantage**
= favorable circumstance
   or situation

centralized   **decentralized**
= brought together in one place
   or under one control

dependent   **independent**
= needing the help of others

PRACTICE EXERCISE

Define the four words in the right-hand column.

H. COMPREHENSION

1. Which people moved out to the suburbs?
2. What are the advantages of suburban living?
3. What are shopping malls?
4. How do the suburbs take advantage of the city?

I. SPEAKING AND WRITING

Discussion

1. Would you rather live in a city, or in a suburb? Why?
2. How can residents of suburbs enjoy the best of both suburb and city?
3. How could a fair arrangement be made between the city and its suburbs?
4. Why would you expect to find more honest local government in the suburbs?

Summary

Briefly tell what you learned about the suburbs.

37

Urban Renewal

Urban Renewal—before and after. One of the buildings restored to its original beauty, in Society Hill, Philadelphia. (Philadelphia Redevelopment Authority)

haphazard	income
factor	tenant
replace	blight
unaided	beautify
scale	raze
undertaking	rehabilitation

As the cities grew, little thought was given to the human effects of their development, or to their beauty. Haphazard growth and other factors led to overcrowding and the rise of slums. The unfortunate conditions of slum life disturbed liberal leaders and writers, and they tried to bring about improvements.

The task of clearing the slums and replacing them with satisfactory,   5
attractive neighborhoods was found to be so costly that the cities could not do it unaided. The United States government has therefore helped the cities in this effort. Starting on a small scale about the time of World War II, the federal government's assistance later expanded into large-scale urban renewal projects available to any city willing to carry out its part of the undertaking. Great sums of   10
money have been spent on a variety of programs. Row upon row of deteriorated houses have been replaced with low-cost modern apartment houses, where rents are kept very low to match the income of the poor tenants. Blighted business areas have been rebuilt attractively. Needed public improvements have been made in transportation and streets, and new schools have been built. Playgrounds and   15
public parks have been set up, and riverfronts have been beautified. As a result, some residents of the suburbs have moved back to the city to enjoy these advantages.

Instead of razing old buildings, some cities have restored interesting structures and neighborhoods. In Philadelphia, for example, Society Hill, a former slum, was made beautiful by the rehabilitation of once-charming houses that   20
date back to Colonial times, but that had been allowed to deteriorate or had been turned into unattractive stores and warehouses. Stripped of nineteenth century additions, these buildings were restored to the simple and harmonious style of the original eighteenth century architecture. This rebuilding was done by private owners over a long period of time, but city planners played an important part in   25
keeping both repairs and new construction in harmony with the character of the neighborhood. The renewed Society Hill is greatly admired by Philadelphians as well as by tourists.

A. PRONUNCIATION

[æ]	versus	[a]
pat		pot
battle		bottle
gnat [næt]		not; knot
hat		hot
band		bond
cat		cot
sad		sod
as		mama
haphazard		papa
factors		father
satisfactory		calm [kam]
attractive		palm [pam]
match		
establish		
standard		
plan		
back		
character		

B. WORD FORMATION

A small group of irregular verbs have this pattern:

PRESENT	ONE-WORD PAST	PAST PARTICIPLE
spend	spent	(have) spent
lend	lent	(have) lent
send	sent	(have) sent
bend	bent	(have) bent
build	built	(have) built

PRACTICE EXERCISE

Fill in each blank with the correct form of the verb. (Remember that the past participle is used only with *have*, *has*, *had*, and in the passive. The base—or present—form of the verb is used with all the other auxiliaries: *did go*, *can see*, *would believe*, etc.)

1. I can't buy any more Christmas presents; I have _____ all my
(spend)
money.

2. Why did you _____ her so much? She will _____ it all
(lend)   (spend)
right away.

3. They _____ the package yesterday.
(send)

4. Our neighbors plan to _____ a garage behind their house.
(build)

5. It was not a serious accident; a fender was _____.
(bend)

C. GRAMMAR

Adverbial clauses of time (beginning with *when, while, before, after, as, until, since*) may come at the beginning of a sentence or at the end.

1. As the cities grew, they developed in haphazard fashion.
   The cities developed in haphazard fashion as they grew.
2. After the slum-dwellings had been torn down, modern apartment houses were built.
   Modern apartment houses were built after the slum-dwellings had been torn down.
3. When the children returned from school, they had no place to play.
   The children had no place to play when they returned from school.
4. Until it received federal help, the city was not able to begin reconstruction.
   The city was not able to begin reconstruction until it received federal help.

D. SPELLING

One way to remember how to spell long words is to say them to yourself, syllable by syllable.

2 SYLLABLES	3 SYLLABLES	6 SYLLABLES
disturbed	fortunate	deterioration
blighted	progressive	rehabilitation
	neighborhood	
	assistance	
	character	
	improvement	

E. PARAPHRASE

FORMAL	COLLOQUIAL
1. little thought was given to	1. nobody bothered about
2. The cities could not do it unaided	2. The cities had to have help.
3. haphazard growth	3. growing every which way
4. They have restored and beautified it.	4. They fixed it up.
5. had been allowed to deteriorate	5. went to the dogs

F. IDIOMS

little thought = hardly any attention
bring about = cause
on a small scale; in a small way = to a limited extent
carry out = accomplish; complete
row upon row = many rows

G. SEMANTICS

1. The auxiliaries **should** and **must** both have to do with obligation. **Should** suggests that the subject has a moral obligation; **must** means that the situation (or something from the outside) makes the action necessary.

should
For the welfare of its people, the city government should clear the slums.
The city should supply its poor citizens with good low-cost housing.
The board of education should improve the schools.

must
Because traffic is always blocked here, they must build a new road.

The cities are not rich enough to rebuild the slums; they must get help from the federal government.

The deteriorated houses are a fire hazard; they must be torn down.

PRACTICE EXERCISE

In the blank write the appropriate auxiliary.

Example:

He felt that he <u>should</u> defend his little brother.
You <u>must</u> have your license with you when you drive.

1. According to the law, you _____ pay your income tax.

2. A seeing person _____ help a blind person to cross the street.

3. Students _____ be honest in taking their exams.

4. A driver _____ stop for a red light.

5. A citizen _____ vote intellligently, after studying the issues and the qualities of the candidates.

6. In some countries a citizen _____ vote; otherwise she or he is fined.

7. If you can't accept their invitation, you _____ explain and express your regrets.

8. A book borrowed from the library _____ be returned within two weeks.

2. Here are some related words, useful in discussing urban renewal:

slum = crowded, poor part of a city
blighted area = a part of the city that has become shabby
ghetto = an undesirable neighborhood into which a minority population is crowded
deteriorate = become worse
rehabilitate = bring back to good condition
restore = bring back to earlier form

H. COMPREHENSION

1. How carefully were the cities planned at the outset?
2. Why did the United States government begin to take part in urban renewal?
3. What is the purpose of low-rent housing?
4. What are the restored neighborhoods?

I. SPEAKING AND WRITING

Discussion

1. Some suburb dwellers have moved back to the cities. Why do you suppose they have done so?
2. Have you seen a restored area in any city? What did it look like?
3. Why do you suppose such strict rules are made for any construction in the restored areas?

Summary

Briefly summarize what you learned about urban renewal.

38

The Puerto Ricans

Puerto Rican self-help: members of the Puerto Rican Community Development Project helping Puerto Rican residents of New York City to register to vote. (Puerto Rican Community Development Project)

large-scale   concerned
mainland   reinforce
seasonal   attain
permanent   civil service
hamper (*verb*)   self-help
altogether   counseling

Puerto Rico became a possession of the United States in 1898, and later a territory. Since 1917 its people have been American citizens. Thus they are free to come to any part of the United States whenever they choose. Large-scale migrations have taken place beginning in 1920, with the greatest influx after World War II. Many Puerto Ricans have arrived in times of high unemployment on their island and job opportunities on the mainland.

Some of them have come as seasonal laborers on the farms of the East, but many moved in as permanent settlers in New York, Philadelphia, Boston, Chicago, and other cities. Their largest community is in East Harlem, a section of New York City, and is known as *El Barrio*. In their crowded neighborhoods the poorer Puerto Ricans live in neglected tenements or houses, with no fit place for the children to play.

Language has been one of the chief problems of the Puerto Ricans, to whom English is foreign. It has prevented many adults from getting desirable jobs. The language problem of Puerto Rican children has also been serious because it has hampered many of them at school. Being afraid of failure there, some children become truants and get into trouble; others drop out of school altogether. The boards of education of New York, Philadelphia, and other cities have been concerned about this problem for some time, and have developed Spanish–English programs in the schools of Puerto Rican neighborhoods. Specially trained teachers are employed for English instruction; and during the early years of school, Spanish is used as the language for learning arithmetic and other basic subjects.

The federal Bilingual Act of 1968 ruled that every school with a group of twenty-five or more pupils whose language is other than English must arrange a bilingual program for them in their own language as well as in English. This act reinforced and greatly increased bilingual education for Spanish-speakers and others.

Although many Puerto Ricans in the United States work in factories, hotels, and hospitals, some have attained civil-service positions, especially in the U.S. Postal Service. Those who have acquired higher education have entered various professions, including teaching, social work, law, and medicine. Some

have succeeded as writers, actors, and athletes. There are Puerto Rican officials in
the city and state governments, and their first representative was elected to the
United States Congress in 1970.

Perhaps the most encouraging fact of Puerto Rican life here is the establishment of a number of self-help organizations. An outstanding example is
Aspira (with chapters in New York, Philadelphia, Chicago, and Miami), which
aims to develop leadership among Puerto Rican youth. It finds them summer jobs
and part-time work during the school year. It offers educational and employment
counseling, financial aid, and even English instruction. The Spanish Merchants
Association gives technical assistance and loans to small businesses. The National
Congress for Puerto Rican Civil Rights helps in legal matters, housing, labor
problems, and job placement. Through these and other organizations, Puerto
Ricans who have attained success give their time and energy as well as financial
help for the betterment of their people.

A. PRONUNCIATION

Practice pronouncing these words.

> Chicago [šI ka′gow]
> corps [kɔr]
> business [bIz′ nIs]
> government [gʌv′ər mənt]
> bilingual
> opportunity
> truant
> permanent
> altogether
> neglected

B. WORD FORMATION

Self is a reflexive prefix that attaches with a hyphen and forms many nouns and
adjectives.

NOUNS

self-help = work that solves one's own problems
self-respect = maintenance of one's own dignity
self-defense = protection or resistance against attack

ADJECTIVES

self-sufficient = able to supply one's own needs
self-reliant = depending on one's own powers
self-important = having an exaggerated idea of one's own importance
self-evident = clear in itself, even without proof
self-made = having succeeded by oneself, without the help of others

NOUN	ADJECTIVE
self-confidence	self-confident
self-criticism	self-critical
self-control	self-controlled

PRACTICE EXERCISE

Fill in each blank, choosing from the lists of nouns and adjectives formed with the prefix **self**.

1. She was calm when she came on the stage; her acting experience had made her _____.

2. The fact is _____; you don't have to convince them.

3. The lawyer argued that the defendant had hit the man in _____.

4. In modern life hardly anyone is _____, producing everything for him- or herself.

5. To break a bad habit, one must have _____.

6. He became a success by his own efforts and is proud of being a _____ man.

7. Everyone dislikes a _____ person.

8. _____ helps a person to improve.

C. GRAMMAR

1. An adjective modifying the noun or pronoun that precedes it is often combined with an infinitive referring to that adjective. The modified noun or pronoun represents the person(s) associated with the action of the infinitive.

Puerto Ricans are **free to come** here.
The man is **ready to work**.
He was a good student, **eager to learn**.
They were **willing to help** their neighbor.
The boy, **afraid to fly**, went by train.
I am **happy to be** here.

2.   There is a similar pattern with **too** modifying the adjective.

too tired to play
too bright to fail
too bored to listen
too frightened to speak
too sick to go

PRACTICE EXERCISE

Make up a sentence for each of the five **too** phrases listed in section C2.

Examples:

The sick man was *too weak to walk* alone.
We thought they were *too smart to make* such a foolish mistake.

D. SPELLING

Some common words have unusual spellings for their vowel sound.

ea for [ey]	**eigh** for [ey]	**ove** for [uwv]	**eo** for [iy]
great	eight	move	people
break	freight	prove	
steak	neighbor	improve	
	weigh		

E. PARAPHRASE

FORMAL	COLLOQUIAL
1. large-scale migration	1. wholesale migration
2. a neglected building	2. a building in bad shape
3. whenever they choose	3. anytime they feel like it
4. have been concerned about it	4. are worried about it

F. IDIOMS

take place = happen
free to come = allowed to come as one wishes
in times of unemployment = when many are unemployed
know-how = skill; an understanding of a technique

G. SEMANTICS

permanent = long-lasting; enduring
temporary = for a time only; for a short while
frequent = often; at short intervals
occasional = happening now and then; once in a while
rare = coming far apart in time; unusual

H. COMPREHENSION

1. What conditions made unusually large numbers of Puerto Ricans come to the mainland at certain times?
2. What and where is *El Barrio*?
3. What have the federal government agencies been doing for Puerto Ricans?
4. How have some Puerto Ricans advanced themselves?
5. What do the Puerto Ricans' self-help organizations do?

I. SPEAKING AND WRITING

Discussion

1. Why is it incorrect to refer to the Puerto Ricans as immigrants?
2. In what kinds of work is knowing the language not very important? Give examples and explain why.
3. Have you ever been in a place where you didn't know the language at all? How does it feel?
4. If the children are allowed to forget their native tongue, how does that affect their family life?
5. Why are self-help activities so important?

Summary

Briefly tell what you learned about the Puerto Ricans.

39

Alaska, the Arctic State

Alaska scenery—glacier in Mount McKinley National Monument. (National Park Service, Department of Interior)

persuade
recognize
wisdom
purchase
folly
peak

vast
glacier [gley′ šər]
contrast
ancient [eyn′ šənt]
arctic
dairy

Alaska became the forty-ninth state of the United States in 1958. Ninety years earlier Secretary of State Seward had with great difficulty persuaded the Congress to buy it from Russia for $15,000,000. For many years people who failed to recognize the wisdom of this purchase called Alaska "Seward's Folly."

Alaska is the largest of the states in area, but the smallest in population. It has magnificent scenery with high mountains, including the highest peak in North America, and vast glaciers. Where the Alaskan Peninsula begins, there is the remarkable Valley of Ten Thousand Smokes, where steaming volcanic vapors rise constantly. There are also interesting animals on land and in the sea, including polar bears, reindeer, wolves, seals, and whales.

It is a land of great contrasts. In the treeless, snow-covered north, Eskimo tribes live by hunting seals and polar bears and keep up the ancient customs and crafts of their ancestors. But farther south there are modern cities with tall buildings and fashionable homes. People and goods come and go by airline, railroad, and automobile. There is a fine educational system, including universities and two-year colleges.

Alaska also has great contrasts in climate. While the northern part, within the Arctic Circle, is bitter cold, the south, near Canada, is damp and mild. Even in the central part there are some places warm enough for dairy and vegetable farming.

The population of Alaska was only 200,000 at the time of its purchase, but it grew very fast, especially after gold was discovered in the Yukon Valley in 1897. After the end of that gold rush many Americans continued to move to Alaska nevertheless, in search of opportunities on the new frontier of the United States.

A. PRONUNCIATION

Vowels in unstressed syllables tend to become [ə]. These syllables are briefly and lightly pronounced. English has stress-timed rhythm; the unstressed syllables are crowded together and pronounced quickly, and the stressed syllables are approximately equally spaced in time. Practice the following and other long words to understand this effect.

difficulty	**veg**etable [vɛj'tə bəl]
mag**nif**icent	es**pe**cially
mountainous	oppor**tu**nity
interesting	ob**jec**tionable

B. WORD FORMATION

In the comparison of adjectives, **-er** (meaning 'more') and **-est** (meaning 'most') are added to one-syllable adjectives and to adjectives ending in **-y** (after changing their final **-y** to **-i**).

higher	highest		happier	happiest
finer	finest		earlier	earliest
nearer	nearest		sillier	silliest
closer	closest		thriftier	thriftiest
greater	greatest		lovelier	loveliest

C. GRAMMAR

A verb of request, command, etc., may be followed by an infinitive that tells what is to be done. Between the verb and the infinitive there is a noun or pronoun naming the one who is to do the action stated in the infinitive.

> persuaded the Congress to buy it
> told the children to go home

Note that in this pattern *ask* means 'request', and *tell* means 'order' or 'command'.

PRACTICE EXERCISE

Fill in the blanks in the following expressions. (Note that the form of the verb may be changed to the past tense or another tense as necessary.)

Example:

invited his <u>friends</u> to <u>join</u> him

1. convince _____ to _____

2. urge _____ to _____

3. ask _____ to _____

4. request _____ to _____

5. beg _____ to _____

6. advise _____ to _____

7. tell _____ to _____

8. order _____ to _____

9. command _____ to _____

D. SPELLING

Common spellings for the [iy] sound.

ee	ea	e-*consonant*-e
peek	peak	scene
deer	dear	concrete
meet	meat	interfere
week	weak	sincere
feet	feat	here
see	sea	complete

Look up the meanings of any of these words that you do not know. Notice the pairs of words that sound alike but have different meanings, like *seen* and *scene*, *meet* and *meat*.

E. PARAPHRASE

	FORMAL	COLLOQUIAL
1.	vapors rise constantly	smoke comes up all the time
2.	persuade someone	{ sell someone the idea / talk someone into it
3.	failed to recognize	{ didn't get the idea / didn't catch on
4.	The population increased rapidly.	The population { boomed / was upped fast.
5.	Gold was discovered.	They found gold.

F. IDIOMS

live by hunting = support oneself by hunting
keep up = continue; maintain

G. SEMANTICS

Words of related meaning:

> **huge** = very large in size or bulk
> **vast** = very large in area or extent
> **tremendous** = impressively big
> **great** = large in importance or size
> **magnificent** = impressively beautiful; grand
>
> **wet** = watery
> **damp** = slightly wet throughout
> **humid** = wet (refers to air)

PRACTICE EXERCISE

Select an appropriate word from the list in section G to complete each sentence.

1. A _____ level field lay before her, as far as she could see.

2. From the top of the hill they admired the _____ view.

3. His birthday is celebrated as a national holiday because he was a _____ man.

4. Elephants are _____ animals.

5. Those _____ trucks can carry _____ loads.

6. Tourists are impressed by this _____ mansion.

H. COMPREHENSION

1. Why did people call Alaska "Seward's Folly?"
2. What interesting scenery can be seen there?
3. How is the northern part different from the south?
4. How does Alaska compare with the other states of the United States in area and in population?

I. SPEAKING AND WRITING

Discussion

1. Do you know what a secretary of state does?
2. Was Alaska a bargain? Why?
3. Which part of Alaska would you consider most interesting to visit?
4. If you were to move to Alaska, which part would you rather live in?

Summary

In your own words, tell what you have learned about Alaska.

40
Hawaii, the Beautiful

Scenic beauty of Hawaii—one of its many lovely beaches. (Hawaii Visitors Bureau)

volcano	export
lava	altitude
eruption	exceptionally
fertile	secular
thrive	research

Hawaii, a group of islands located about 2,400 miles west of California, became the fiftieth state of the United States of America in 1959. The islands contain many volcanoes, some of which erupt from time to time. The lava that flowed from earlier eruptions has developed into very fertile soil. Many plants thrive there, particularly sugar, pineapples, and tropical flowers. Hawaii prospers by exporting all of these and also by tourism. Tourists are attracted by the beautiful scenery and the sunny beaches. Hawaii is particularly fortunate in its climate, which, although it varies at different altitudes, is exceptionally mild for a tropical region.

The first schools in Hawaii were those established by missionaries; today most of the schools are secular, and education is compulsory. One of Hawaii's centers of higher learning is the University of Hawaii, established in 1907. It is a large university with modern research facilities.

The people of Hawaii are noted for their friendliness and charm. The population is basically Polynesian, with much intermarriage. There are also many Japanese and other Far Eastern people who settled there, and about twenty-five percent of the people are Caucasians (whites). These varied racial and ethnic groups have learned to live together in peace and harmony, setting an example well worth following.

A. PRONUNCIATION

Personal pronouns are stressed less than nouns in the same position. Pronouns as objects of verbs or prepositions are weak in stress.

Hawaii exports píneapples. Hawaii expórts thĕm.
The scenery is beaútiful; tourists enjóy ĭt.
The people are fríendly; visitors like to tálk with thĕm.
It's a goód boók; I líke ĭt.
Did you búy ĭt?
I loóked for hĕr, but I didn't sée hĕr there.

B. WORD FORMATION

Notice how the vowel changes in these very common irregular verbs.

PRESENT	ONE-WORD PAST	PAST PARTICIPLE
thrive	throve (or, thrived)	(have) thriven
drive	drove	(have) driven
ride	rode	(had) ridden
write	wrote	(had) written

Many longer, less commonly used verbs are regular. The past and the past participle end in **-ed** and the vowel does not change.

decide	decided	(have) decided
arrive	arrived	(has) arrived
describe	described	(had) described
revive	revived	(have) revived

PRACTICE EXERCISE

Choose the correct form for each verb.

1. In ancient times many plants _____ there, but today it is a desert.
   (thrive)

2. He has never _____ a truck before.
   (drive)

3. We were in front, and the children _____ in the back of the car.
   (ride)

4. I must _____ an answer to her letter.
   (write)

5. They _____ to go by bus.
   (decide)

6. The guests have already _____.
   (arrive)

7. The author _____ the scene very clearly.
   (describe)

8. They _____ the woman who had fainted.
   (revive)

C. GRAMMAR

The degree of a modifier and the consequent effect or result of that modifier are shown by the following structure:

so (adjective or adverb) **that** (consequence)

ADJECTIVE

It is **so beautiful that** many tourists come to see it.
The weather is **so mild that** one can swim the year round.
The flowers are **so lovely that** they are imported by mainland United States.

ADVERB

He swam **so well that** he won in the competition.
It rains **so rarely that** you need not take an umbrella.
They sang **so beautifully that** the audience was delighted.

PRACTICE EXERCISE

Make up a sentence for each of the following expressions.

Examples:

The children were *so frightened that* they began to cry.
He had driven there *so frequently that* he knew the way.

1. so cold that
2. so joyful that
3. so tired that
4. so strong that
5. so disappointed that
6. so kind that
7. so carefully that
8. so often that

D. SPELLING

The letters **ch** represent the sound [k] in words taken from classical Greek.

school	cholera
scholar	chrome

scholastic	chromatic
chord	Christian
chorus	Christmas
character	architecture
chronic	archaic
chronological	orchestra

E. PARAPHRASE

FORMAL	COLLOQUIAL
1. Education is compulsory.	1. You have to go to school.
2. are noted for their friendliness	2. are known as particularly friendly
3. These varied groups have learned to live together in harmony.	3. These different groups get along fine.
4. The population is basically Polynesian.	4. The people are mostly Polynesian. / Most of the people are Polynesian.
5. has developed into fertile soil	5. got to be rich soil

F. IDIOMS

from time to time = occasionally
well worth while = good enough to repay one's time or attention
setting an example = being a model
get along with = be on good terms with
the year round = at all seasons of the year; throughout the year

G. SEMANTICS

Words of related meaning:

thrive = develop successfully (often used to refer to plants)
    Pineapples thrive in Hawaii.
prosper = flourish; be successful (usually about economic matters)
    The immigrants prospered in their new land.
grow = increase by natural development; get larger

H. COMPREHENSION

1. What was Hawaii's soil made of?
2. Why do people travel to Hawaii?
3. What kinds of schools are there in Hawaii?
4. What kinds of people live there?

I. SPEAKING AND WRITING

Discussion

1. Would you like to see Hawaii? Why?
2. Hawaii is a favorable place in many ways. What do you consider its most important advantage?
3. Would you like to live in a place with live volcanoes? Why, or why not?

Summary

Tell briefly what kind of place Hawaii is.

41

Civil Rights:
New Horizons
for Blacks

The 1963 March on Washington—part of the assembled crowd. (The Philadelphia Tribune)

horizon	trigger (*verb*)
amendment	widespread
Constitution	protest (*noun*)
racial discrimination	boycott
equality	sit-in
violent	withhold
segregate	skilled
vehicle	white-collar

Blacks are the largest racial minority in the United States. In the 1860s, amendments to the Constitution made these former slaves free and gave them all the rights of citizenship, including the right to vote. However, in the South many whites were determined to keep blacks from enjoying these rights.

The first organization formed for the purpose of improving the condition of black people in the United States was the National Association for the Advancement of Colored People (NAACP). It was founded in 1909 by both white and black leaders to fight against racial discrimination and to work for full political, social, and economic equality. Another organization, the National Urban League, has emphasized employment, job training, education, and housing for blacks.

By the middle of the twentieth century, blacks had made some gains in civil rights and in economic opportunities. A very important step in this direction was the 1954 Supreme Court ruling against separate schools for blacks and for whites. However, many blacks felt that progress was far too slow. Among these was Dr. Martin Luther King, Jr., who believed in nonviolent methods. In 1955 the southern custom of segregating blacks at the back of public vehicles triggered a widespread protest. Under the leadership of Dr. King, a boycott of all the city buses was organized in Montgomery, Alabama. Old and young blacks walked for miles, refusing to ride the buses. Finally the practice of segregating on the buses was stopped.

After this success, King led protests against other forms of segregation in the South. White sympathizers joined blacks in sit-ins in restaurants and other segregated facilities. There were also protest marches. The most impressive of these was a civil rights march in Washington, D.C., in 1963, in which hundreds of thousands of blacks and whites from all parts of the country participated. These protests called to the attention of Americans the unfairness of treating blacks differently because of their race. They helped to bring about further laws abolishing various forms of racial segregation. Included among these are the Civil Rights Act of 1964, which withholds federal funds from school systems that do not integrate their schools, and the Equal Opportunity Act of 1972, which helps blacks to find employment.

In 1964 King was awarded the Nobel peace prize for his contribution to the cause of human rights; later his birthday was made a national holiday in the United States.   35

In recent years blacks have made great progress, especially in education and in government. Many have gone into skilled trades and white-collar jobs. Others have attained high positions in business and the professions. Many blacks have been elected to local as well as to state and national government posts. There are black mayors in many cities, including some of the largest ones.   40

Although all racial problems have not been solved, recent progress in this direction has been quite remarkable.

A. PRONUNCIATION

The [ay] diphthong (often called "long *i*") is pronounced as vowel plus glide.

organize
violent
widespread
mile
finally
why
high
sympathizer

Before a voiceless consonant the diphthong is shorter.

united
life
fight
pipe
bike

SHORTER DIPHTHONG	*versus*	LONGER DIPHTHONG
price		prize
rice		rise
right		ride
sight		side
knife		knives
white		wide

B. WORD FORMATION

Some pairs of noun and verb of the same root have the same form and the same pronunciation.

	NOUN	VERB
gain	They made an important gain.	He will gain a huge profit.
trigger	A gun has a trigger.	A small incident can trigger a widespread protest.
rule	You must obey the rule.	The courts must rule on this matter.
talk	He gave us an interesting talk on local politics.	They talk too much.

Similarly, the following words may be used as a noun or as a verb.

march	riot
drive	wave
end	shock
honor	murder
prize	race

GRAMMAR

The verbs **say** and **tell** contrast in the structures in which they are used.

1. The object of **say** consists of the words that were actually said (a quotation) or a noun that represents the words that were said. **Say** never has an indirect object (dative).

DIRECT QUOTATION

He said, "Let us boycott the bus line."
They said, "We'll walk instead of riding."

INDIRECT QUOTATION

He said that they should boycott the bus line.
They said that they would walk instead of riding.

REPRESENTATION OF QUOTATION

He said those words.
They said it.
She said anything that came to her mind.

2.   Tell has two objects: an indirect object indicating to whom the information is given, and a direct object indicating the information (content) or the form of information.

INDIRECT   DIRECT OBJECT

He told them the truth.

INDIRECT DIRECT OBJECT

They will tell us what they know.

INDIRECT   DIRECT OBJECT

She tells him an interesting story.

INDIRECT   DIRECT OBJECT

They told Mary the news.

PRACTICE EXERCISE

Supply the missing word in each sentence (**say**, **said**, **tell**, **told**).

Examples:

The child told them everything.
Jim said "Let's go, or we'll be late."

1. He _____ me the story.

2. She _____ that she was tired.

3. They _____, "We must go home now."

4. Jim _____ us all about the accident.

5. We _____ them the important facts.

6. He _____ that he will come back tomorrow.

7. They _____, "Hello!"

8. Jane _____ everybody the secret.

9. All the witnesses _____ that they had seen him there.

10. The sign _____, "No smoking."

D. SPELLING

Don't confuse these pairs of words which sound alike but are spelled differently.

1. peace (= tranquility)	piece
2. their (= belonging to them)	there
3. too (= also)	to
4. buy (= purchase)	by
5. write (as with pen, pencil)	right
6. sew (= stitch)	so
7. hire (= employ)	higher
8. whole (= entire)	hole
9. its (= belonging to it)	it's (it is)

PRACTICE EXERCISE

Write the correct word in each blank.

Examples:

He believes in <u>peace</u>, not war.
We walk <u>there</u> every Sunday.
He likes skiing and skating, <u>too</u>.

1. Did you _____ them a present?
       (buy, by)

2. He hurt his _____ leg when he fell.
       (write, right)

3. Her mother taught her to _____.
       (sew, so)

4. A mountain is _____ than a hill.
       (hire, higher)

5. She read the _____ book in three days.
       (whole, hole)

6. _____ a beautiful day; let's take a walk.
   (Its, It's)

E. PARAPHRASE

FORMAL	COLLOQUIAL
1. determined to keep them from enjoying	1. set on not letting them have
2. for the purpose of improving the condition (of)	2. to make it better (for)
3. their progress was far too slow	3. they didn't move nearly fast enough
4. his contribution to the cause of human rights	4. what he did for human rights

F. IDIOMS

give in = yield; admit defeat; stop opposing

call to their attention = make them notice; make them aware

make progress
make headway } = move forward; advance

G. SEMANTICS

Here are a few of the adverbs that begin a sentence or a clause, linking it to what came before. These adverbs relate the sentence to the information contained in the preceding sentences.

furthermore = in addition; besides

moreover = beyond what has been said

however = yet, in spite of what has been said before

therefore = as a result

H. COMPREHENSION

1. What did the constitutional amendments of the 1860s do for blacks?
2. What is the purpose of the NAACP?
3. What were Dr. King's nonviolent methods of fighting racial discrimination?
4. What beneficial results followed from the 1963 civil rights march?
5. In what ways have blacks progressed?

I. SPEAKING AND WRITING

Discussion

1. Why do you suppose many whites have joined blacks in civil rights demonstrations?
2. Do you think that some blacks are more dissatisfied and impatient now that great gains have already been made? Why, or why not?
3. If people feel that they are being treated unjustly, is it better to complain and be angry, or to demonstrate and call attention to their problems?

Summary

Briefly state what you have learned about blacks and civil rights.

42

The Feminist Movement

Woman cable-splicer on a repair job for Bell Telephone. (Bell Telephone of Pennsylvania)

dependent   bar (*verb*)
deprived   career
privilege   equality
status   restricted
activist   focus (*verb*)
participant   role
denounce   assign

Although the women's rights movement in the United States is thought of as a recent development, its beginnings date back a century and a half. At that time women were dependents in the eyes of the law, and they were deprived of the rights and privileges of adults. A woman had no property rights, even over what she had inherited or over any wages that she earned. Decisions about family matters and about the children were made by her husband, the "head of the family."

The first public protests against the low status of women were made in the 1830s. In 1848 the leaders of this movement (some of whom were antislavery activists as well) assembled the first Women's Rights Convention, demanding equality. In this struggle as well as in the long, hard fight for women's suffrage, the participants were jeered at and insulted. They were denounced as immoral, and their ideas were considered dangerous to society.

Nevertheless, by 1900 women had won the right to vote in several states, and in 1920 the Nineteenth Amendment to the Constitution granted them suffrage throughout the United States. By that time many women were attending college, and increasing numbers were entering professions that had previously been barred to women. A limited number of women even held high academic and government positions. In spite of all this progress, careers for women were largely restricted to teaching, nursing, and office work.

The Feminist movement, which developed during the 1960s, has focused on economic rights such as "equal pay for equal work." In addition some groups have stressed psychological and social equality. The main purpose of this movement is to free women from the restricted role that society assigned to them. It seeks to enable them to choose between a career and the home—or to choose a combination of the two. It claims that society as a whole would benefit if every person were allowed to develop his or her abilities fully and to use them to the full. The Feminist movement believes that the statement in the United States Declaration of Independence, "all men are created equal" really means "all human beings are created equal."

A. PRONUNCIATION

Words for pronunciation attention.

woman [wʊ′ mən]
women [wɪ mɪn]
psychology [say kal′ ə ji]
psychological [say kə laj′ ɪ kəl]
move [muwv]
prove [pruwv]

B. WORD FORMATION

The prefix **in-** meaning 'not' can be added to certain adjectives to form their opposites. Examples are *indecent*, *insane*, *informal*, *incomplete*. Look up these words, with and without the prefix.
The sound of the prefix blends with the sound which comes after it:

The **n** becomes **m** before **m** or **p** (*immoral*, *impolite*).
The **n** becomes **r** before **r** (*irregular*, *irresistible*).
The **n** becomes **l** before **l** (*illegal*, *illiterate*).

PRACTICE EXERCISE

Following the rules reviewed in section B about the **in-** prefix; write the opposites of these words.

Examples:

distinct   indistinct
legible   illegible
proper   improper

1. patient	8. perfect	15. practical
2. mature	9. correct	16. variable
3. dependent	10. possible	17. logical
4. passable	11. direct	18. exact
5. capable	12. movable	19. personal
6. pure	13. human	20. modest
7. religious	14. responsible	

There is another **in-** prefix, which is based on the preposition-adverb **in** and has the meaning of that preposition-adverb. Examples of words with this prefix are *include, inject, implant, immigration, immerse, inborn, indoor, inside, income, input.*

C. GRAMMAR

1. For some words with noun and verb forms that look alike, the *first* syllable of the noun is stressed, while the *last* syllable of the verb is stressed.

NOUN	VERB
protest	pro**test**
insult	in**sult**
permit	per**mit**
contract	con**tract**
conflict	con**flict**
contrast	con**trast**
rebel	re**bel**
subject	sub**ject**
reject	re**ject**
combine	com**bine**

PRACTICE EXERCISE

In the following sentences, mark the stressed syllable of each underlined word.

Example:

The people are involved in this prótest march because they protest' the new law as unfair.

1. Women first began protesting against their low status in the 1830s.
2. Some people would insult the marchers.
3. You need a permit to enter the military installations.
4. The contract was signed by both people.
5. These ideas conflict with what you said before.
7. The slaves did not rebel.
8. The Constitution states that people must not be subjected to cruel and un-usual punishment.
9. The bargain store sells rejects—products that have been rejected by an inspector at the factory.

10. A <u>combine</u> is a machine that <u>combines</u> the cutting and the threshing processes on farms.

2. A noncount noun (see chapter 11, section C) never has the indefinite article (**a** or **an**). If a limiting or specifying modifier follows the noncount noun, it requires the definite article (**the**).

1. **Discrimination** against any group is wrong.
   The discrimination *practiced by the Klan* harmed the South and the whole nation.
2. The blacks needed **leadership**.
   The leadership *of Dr. King* helped to unite them.
3. **Courage** is a valuable quality.
   The courage *needed to face such dangers* is unusual.
4. She studies **chemistry**.
   The chemistry *that the alchemists practiced* was not scientific.

D. SPELLING

The regular spelling for [ayt] is **-ite**. A special spelling for the same sound is **-ight**. In a few cases the spelling differentiates words that sound alike. Look up *site* and *cite*, which are pronounced like *sight*. (Some advertisements and patented product-names spell *night*, *bright*, and *light* as *nite*, *brite*, and *lite*.)

REGULAR	SPECIAL
bite	right
spite	fight
kite	flight
write	tight
polite	bright
recite	light
quite	might
white	delight

E. PARAPHRASE

FORMAL	COLLOQUIAL
1. was barred to them	1. { was closed to them / They weren't let in.
2. They were ridiculed.	2. People made fun of them.
3. attend college	3. go to college

F. IDIOMS

to the full = as much as possible; completely
in the eyes of = in the opinion of; according to
is thought of as = is considered
dates back to = existed, or began to exist at that time; happened or began
    to happen at that time

G. SEMANTICS

Pairs of words of related meaning:

privilege = special benefit or right
right = what is justly due

jeer = shout insultingly or in ridicule
sneer = show scorn or contempt

immoral = not according to ethical principles; evil
indecent = offending propriety or social standards

H. COMPREHENSION

1. How long ago did protests begin against unfair treatment of women?
2. How did the public react to the protesters?
3. What is "equal pay for equal work"?
4. What do feminists believe about opportunities for women?
5. What is the meaning of "all are created equal"?

I. SPEAKING AND WRITING

Discussion

1. Do you agree with the ideas of the Feminist movement? What is your opinion?
2. Does it seem strange to you that men are working as telephone operators and as teachers of preschool children? Why, or why not?
3. Are men in your parents' native land ashamed to help at home with the children and with housework? How do you feel about that?

4. Do you think that the refrigerator, the vacuum cleaner, and the washing machine have had an effect on women's liberation? How?

Summary

Summarize the reading selection in a few sentences.

43

Ecology:
Rescuing
the Environment

Mass of fish killed by water pollution.

operate

contaminate

depletion

natural resources

alert (*verb*)

environmentalist

interdependence

conservationist

toxic

accumulation

sewage

stringent

emission

exhaust (*noun*)

enforce

regulation

reverse (*verb*)

The conveniences of modern life have brought with them problems that did not exist in the days of simpler living. Machinery that operates on electricity made by burning coal or petroleum is used to process raw materials taken from the earth and to make them into finished products. Gases from these processes rise into the air, producing acid rain, which ruins the forests and pollutes the air as well as bodies of water. Some lakes and rivers have become so contaminated that the fish in them die. In addition to the harm done to those who breathe the polluted air, waste gases have effects on the upper atmosphere, which scientists fear could endanger all life on earth.

These threats, as well as the depletion of natural resources (such as fuels, forests, and soil) by careless, wasteful use, have worried scientists and other thoughtful people. Such persons are also disturbed about the effects of chemical fertilizers and of poisons farmers use in order to destroy insects and weeds. Above all they are alarmed at the interference with the natural balance of the environment, and its possible consequences.

As a result, there have been attempts to alert the public to these dangers. Articles and books have been written by environmentalists and organizations interested in ecology, the study of the interdependence of organisms and the environment.

Federal laws to protect the environment date back to the late nineteenth century, after the conservationists exerted influence to save the forests and other resources from wasteful use and destruction. Later, as modern industry developed, it became necessary to check the harmful emissions, the toxic wastes buried in the ground, and the sewage being emptied into lakes and rivers. Control of automobile exhaust began in California because of special problems there. In the Los Angeles region, because of the particular weather conditions of that area, the exhaust from motor vehicles tends to create a dangerous accumulation of gases called smog. Since the late 1950s California law has enforced the use of antipollution devices on cars, trucks, and buses. During the 1960s and 1970s the federal government ruled increasingly stringent control of emission from motor vehicles, and the states have regular testing of vehicles to enforce limits on exhaust fumes. The United States government's Environmental Protection

Agency (EPA) as well as state agencies have been enforcing regulations on the clearing of dangerous waste dumps, and a national Clean Water Act has been in effect since 1987. One of the Great Lakes, which had been totally polluted, has been returned to a condition fit for fishing and for swimming. Increased attention is also being given to acid rain. Through the use of such antipollution programs it is hoped that the environment can be saved from further deterioration and even that some of the damage can be reversed.

A. PRONUNCIATION

Contrastive stress in a sentence or a word is strong stress on the word or syllable that points out a difference or "carries the information"—even though that word or syllable would not normally be stressed.

> The child learned to tie and *un*tie his shoes.
> In *my* country we have *this* custom, but in *yours* you have a *dif*ferent one.
> That's *Jim's* opinion. What's *Mary's*?
> The *older* child likes *music*; the *younger* one cares only for *foot*ball.

Even articles and prepositions can have contrastive stress.

> This is not just *a* book on the subject; it's *the* book.
> Is it located *near* the corner or *at* the corner?
> You are either *with* us or *against* us.

PRACTICE EXERCISE

Underline the word or the syllable that should have contrastive stress.

1. Don't ask Tom; tell him.
2. Don't ask Tom; ask Bill.
3. Her friends should be for her—not against her.
4. My books are on the desk, but hers are all over the place.
5. Should the comma come before the quotation mark or after it?
6. He is not just an authority in the field; he is the authority.
7. Hawaii grows pineapples and exports them.
8. The northern part is cold, but the south is warm.
9. She didn't actually see it; she just imagined it.
10. In my country people marry earlier than in your country.

B. WORD FORMATION

1.   The prefix **inter-** means 'between' or 'mutual'.

   interdepedence = depending on each other
   interference = coming between
   international = between nations

PRACTICE EXERCISE

Look up the following words in the dictionary, and make up sentences for any six of them.

   Example:

   This corporation conducts *international* trade.

   interchangeable   intermediary
   interconnect   intermittent
   interject   interrupt
   interlock   interval
   intermarry   interview

2.   The noun suffix **-cide** means 'killer' or 'killing'.

   germicide = germ-killer
   insecticide = insect-killer
   homicide = the killing of one human being by another
   genocide = the extermination of an entire people

C. GRAMMAR

When **-ing** words derived from verbs are used as nouns, they are called gerunds. The gerund of a transitive verb can take an object. The subject may be in possessive form or may be omitted.

1. They breathe the polluted air, and they become ill.
   Breathing the polluted air makes them ill.
   Their breathing the polluted air makes them ill.
2. The farmers spray insecticides; this can harm the birds.
   Spraying insecticides can harm the birds.
   The farmers' spraying insecticides can harm the birds.

3. People celebrate Earth Day; this reminds them of the need to protect the environment.
    Celebrating Earth Day reminds people . . .
    People's celebrating Earth Day reminds them . . .
4. Natural resources are wasted; conservationists try to reduce that.
    Conservationists try to reduce the wasting of natural resources.

D. SPELLING

Some words end in a consonant followed by **le**. (The **le** is pronounced [əl] just like the **el** in *label, shovel*.)

able	settle	bubble
table	bottle	trouble
cable	battle	uncle
little	rattle	handle

E. PARAPHRASE

FORMAL	COLLOQUIAL
1. its possible consequences	1. what might happen as a result
2. attempting to alert the public to these dangers	2. trying to warn people
3. increasingly stringent controls	3. tougher curbs
4. prevent them from deteriorating further	4. keep them from getting worse

F. IDIOMS

it is hoped = one hopes
as a result = consequently
in a fog = confused
break your word = not keep your promise

G. SEMANTICS

1. There are several kinds of auxiliaries of obligation (see chapter 37, section G) in the negative.

1. Obligation not to do something
    a. Moral obligation to avoid doing something—**should not, shouldn't**

Factories should not pour harmful waste into streams.
People should not burn leaves on dry, windy days.
The child should not disobey his parents.
You shouldn't break your word.

  b. Obligation to avoid doing something because of a law or another outside force—**must not, mustn't**
  You must not drive a car without a license.
  She mustn't go back into the burning house.
  They must not hurt the child.
  He mustn't leave the hospital until the doctor permits it.

2. Lack of obligation (not obliged to)—**do not have to, don't have to**
  You don't have to pay until the end of the month.
  They didn't have to thank us.
  A child under six years old doesn't have to attend school.
  On weekends she doesn't have to get up early.

2. Closely related weather words:

mist = tiny drops of water suspended in the air just above the ground
fog = thick mist
smog = mixture of smoke and fog; polluted air

H. COMPREHENSION

1. What pollutes the air?
2. What harm can air pollution do?
3. What products used in farming can harm the environment? How?
4. What important step did the government of California take?
5. What is the federal government doing about protecting the environment?

I. SPEAKING AND WRITING

Discussion

1. Do you think it was better in preindustrial times when people didn't have to worry about pollution?
2. Why is it important for people to know about these dangers?
3. What can you do to help protect the environment, even in a small way?

Summary

Briefly summarize the reading selection.

44

The National Parks

Parks for People—a hiker on the Appalachian Trail enjoying the beauty of the Great Smoky Mountains National Park, Tennessee. (National Park Service)

generation

lumber

mine (*noun* and *verb*)

abandon

slaughter

wildlife

wilderness

geyser

variety

scenery

grove

gorge (*noun*)

recreation

preserve (*verb*)

The early settlers of the United States, and many generations after them, found their land so rich in natural resources that they did not think of conserving them. Forests—a problem for the new settlers—were cut down for lumber as well as to clear land for farming, with no attempt to plant new trees. Minerals were mined carelessly, and the mines were abandoned with much valuable ore left in them. The buffalo and other animals were thoughtlessly slaughtered, sometimes for no purpose but sport. There was such a wealth of resources and of open space that they were believed to be endless.

It was not until the late 1800s that some wise Americans, including President Theodore Roosevelt, began to think in terms of conservation. They worried about the loss to future generations of natural resources and wildlife and of the beauty of the wilderness. One result of their efforts was the establishment in 1872 of Yellowstone Park, which extends through parts of the states of Wyoming, Montana, and Idaho. This park is an impressive area of 3,500 square miles of forested mountain country with remarkable scenery. The Yellowstone River has cut a deep canyon between steep walls of colored rock. At the head of this canyon the river drops in a high waterfall. Yellowstone Park is the world's largest area of geysers, and it includes many hot springs. There is also a rich variety of plants and animals.

Many other national parks have been established, and since 1916 they have been under the care of the National Park Service, a part of the United States Department of the Interior. One of the most famous of these is Yosemite Park in California, containing mountains, lakes, and waterfalls. Here one finds groves of ancient giant sequoia trees. The highest is 209 feet tall and almost 35 feet in diameter. Its age is estimated to be more than 3,000 years.

Perhaps the most dramatic scenery of all is that of the Grand Canyon National Park. The 300-mile gorge cut by the Colorado River is 4,000 to 6,000 feet deep. It is lined with magnificent walls of sculpture-like rocks, whose colors change with the light of the sun.

Today the National Park Service maintains over thirty million acres of public parklands and hundreds of national shrines and recreation areas. These are well equipped for camping and hiking as well as other outdoor activities. The parks exist for the enjoyment of all visitors, both American and foreign. And they preserve some of the natural beauty of the United States for the benefit and pleasure of future generations.

A. PRONUNCIATION

Practice words for special pronunciation.

resources [ri sɔrs′ əz]
slaughter [slɔ′ tər]
geyser [gay′ zər]
variety [və ray′ ə ti]
Yosemite [yow sɛ′ mə ti]
sequoia [sɪ kwoy′ ə]
diameter [day æm′ ə tər]
ancient [eyn′ šənt]
scenery [siy′ nə ri]
recreation [rɛk ri ey′ šən]
foreign [far′ɪn], [fɔr′ɪn]

B. WORD FORMATION

Short verbs ending in **t** are very important because many of them are so common. These verbs should be studied in three categories, according to how they form their past tense.

1.   A few short verbs ending in **t** keep exactly the same form in the present (base form), the one-word past, and the past participle (after *have*, *had*, etc.).

PRESENT	PAST	PAST PARTICIPLE
cut	cut	(have) cut
put	put	(have) put
let	let	(have) let
bet	bet	(have) bet
set	set	(have) set
hit	hit	(have) hit
quit	quit	(have) quit
cost	cost	(have) cost
hurt	hurt	(have) hurt
burst	burst	(have) burst
shut	shut	(have) shut

With all these verbs the single-consonant **t** is doubled before **-ing**: *cutting*, *putting*, *letting*, etc.

2.   A second group of verbs ending in **t** change their vowels in the past forms. For example:

PRESENT	PAST	PAST PARTICIPLE
sit	sat	(have) sat
get	got	(have) gotten
meet	met	(have) met
eat	ate	(have) eaten
shoot	shot	(have) shot

3.   Many short verbs ending in **t** are regular, that is, they form the past tense as well as the past participle with the ending **-ed**.

fit	fitted	(have) fitted
rot	rotted	(have) rotted
lift	lifted	(have) lifted
bat	batted	(have) batted
knit	knitted	(have) knitted

PRACTICE EXERCISE

Write the correct form of the verb in each blank.

1. Last week he _____ his job.
     (quit)

2. Food _____ more in this store.
     (cost)

3. She has already _____ her breakfast.
     (eat)

4. The hunter _____ the deer, but he didn't kill it.
     (shoot)

5. She _____ the heavy rock.
     (lift)

6. We _____ in the bus yesterday.
     (meet)

7. They _____ there until their mother came for them.
     (sit)

8. The child cried when her balloon _____ .
     (burst)

9. When Jim comes home, he always _____ his coat in the closet.
                                                    (put)

10. I think I _____ the answer right.
                    (get)

C. GRAMMAR

1. **If**-clauses stating a supposition that is not true or not real use a form of the verb that looks like the one-word past (although it deals with the present time). The other clause of the sentence uses **would** as auxiliary. Note that the **if**-clause may come at the beginning or at the end of the sentence.

> If I **had** the time [*but I don't*], I **would** visit Yellowstone.
> If they **believed** in conservation [*but they don't*], they **would** be careful to avoid polluting the air.
> If you **appreciated** the beauty of the scenery [*but you don't*], you **would** enjoy this trip.
> She **would** speak English well by now if she **attended** classes every day.
> We **would** tell you the answer if we **knew** it.

2. With the **be** verb, the form **were** is used with all subjects for unreal supposition in present time.

> If I **were** you, I **would** go there.
> If it **were** sunny today, they **would** be outdoors.
> If you **were** a millionaire, **would** you buy it?
> If she **were** here, she **would** help us.

3. The same forms of the verb are used for expressing an unreal or hopeless wish for the present time. (The word **that** may be used after the first verb but is not necessary.)

> I wish (that) I **had** the time to visit Yellowstone.
> He wishes (that) he **knew** the answer.
> Jim wishes (that) he **were** a millionaire.
> I wish (that) I **were** you.
> I wish (that) it **were** sunny today.

PRACTICE EXERCISE

Complete the following sentences.

Examples:

If I knew the answer, I <u>would tell you</u>.
If they were honest, they <u>would admit their misdeed</u>.

1. If she talked English all the time, she _____.

2. If Jim drove carefully, he _____.

3. If you really knew them, you _____.

4. If you practiced the music every day, you _____.

5. If I were rich, _____.

6. If Mary were a loyal friend, _____.

7. If I were you, _____.

8. If he were smart, _____.

9. Mary wishes (that) she _____.

10. I wish (that) _____.

D. SPELLING

Words for special spelling attention:

valuable	recreation
scenery	geyser
slaughter	pleasure

E. PARAPHRASE

FORMAL	COLLOQUIAL
1. with no attempt to replant	1. didn't try to plant new ones
2. a rich variety	2. lots of different kinds
3. were thoughtlessly slaughtered	3. They killed them right and left.
4. most dramatic scenery	4. gorgeous views
5. gave no thought to	5. didn't pay any attention to
6. they had no thought of it.	6. It never entered their minds.

F. IDIOMS

under the care of = being taken care of; being managed by
without limit = endless
for the benefit of _____ = to be good for _____
rich in _____ = well-equipped with _____
in terms of = with respect to; in relation to
for no purpose but sport = just for sport

G. SEMANTICS

Three verbs relating to conservation:

conserve = use carefully and wisely so as to keep something in good condition and not waste it
maintain = keep in good repair under careful management
preserve = keep something in its original condition, not letting it decay; make it last or endure

H. COMPREHENSION

1. Why were earlier generations careless in dealing with natural resources?
2. What was President Theodore Roosevelt's attitude?
3. What was the first success of the conservationists?
4. What do you expect to see in Yellowstone Park?
5. What are the sequoias noted for?
6. Why are the national parks important for the future?

I. SPEAKING AND WRITING

Discussion

1. Many lumber companies, cattle ranchers, and other business concerns have objected to reserving lands for national parks and other conservation areas. Do you agree with them?
2. Is it surprising that the first conservationists began to worry about loss of resources and open space at so early a time? Why?

Summary

Briefly tell what you have learned about the national parks.

American Terms

These terms frequently appear in American newspapers and magazines and are often used on television and radio, but they have not all been used in this text.

assembly line   arrangement for assembling a product by having each worker perform a successive (following) step on it

baby sitter   one who takes care of a child when the parents are absent

bail out   jump out by parachute; release or rescue a person who is in trouble

barn-raising   a party for neighbors who have built a barn together

bayou   outlet of a river, particularly of the Mississippi near New Orleans

blacklist   list (usually, secret) of persons disapproved of and to be disfavored

blue-collar workers   unskilled or semiskilled wage earners

blue laws   restrictive laws based on strict religious rules of conduct

boom   unusual economic prosperity; the opposite is *bust*

bootlegging   dealing illegally in liquor or in other goods

brain trust   a group of experts who are consultants for the president or other government officials

brass (or **top brass**)   high-ranking military officers

carpetbagger   an outsider who comes to take unfair advantage of a situation, particularly some northerners in the South after the Civil War

caucus   meeting of the leaders of a party to decide on unified action

chain store   a retail store that is part of a combined group of stores owned and managed together

civil service   postal and other nonmilitary services; candidates for civil service positions in the United States are chosen by competitive examinations

closed shop   place of work that hires union members only

cold war   intense enmity between nations without actual fighting

company union   a labor union dominated by the employer

con man (or **confidence man**)   one who swindles his victims after gaining their confidence

conscientious objector   one who refuses to fight in war because of religious or ethical principles

conservation   preservation and careful use of natural resources

cover-up (*noun*)   actions to hide wrongdoing

dark horse   a candidate who was not known before

269

deal (or **secret deal**)   private arrangement for the participants' own benefit, not for the good of the public

depression (**economic**)   period of slowing of the economy, with business losses and unemployment

discrimination   prejudice against persons, or unfair treatment because of race, religion, etc.

dust bowl   farmland eroded by wind, especially in the Great Plains

eat crow   to have to retract what one has said; to be humiliated

ecology   relation between organisms and their environment; conservationists are particularly interested in ecology

executive branch   the president, his cabinet, and the agencies working for them in the federal government; in the states, the governor and his staff, etc.·

expense account   personal expenditures of an employee, for which the employer is expected to pay

filibuster   a very long speech, made in a legislative body in order to delay action and prevent passing a law

fringe benefit   extra advantage in addition to wages

go to bat for   defend; take someone's part

graft   money acquired dishonestly through a person's political position or power

grandstand play   an action just to draw attention or to impress

grass roots   the ordinary people of an area, whose opinion is politically important

greenhorn   a naive, inexperienced person; a new immigrant

gripe   complain

(in on the) ground floor   at an advantage because of having been there from the start

hard hat   a construction worker, especially a politically conservative one

head start   advantage gained by being early

hideout   a remote hiding place of lawbreakers (outlaws, criminals)

hit   a popular success

hogan   Navaho Indian house made of branches covered with earth

hoodwink   deceive

hooked   addicted, particularly to drugs

hooky   unjustified absence from school

inaugural   taking office (ceremony for beginning in the new position)

Indian summer   period of warm dry weather in late fall in some parts of the U.S.

inner city   central part of city with poor residence area

inside track   favored position, with special advantage

judicial branch   branch of the government having courts of justice for settling disputes and interpreting the law

Jim Crow   the former southern practice of segregating blacks in public places

lame duck   official who is finishing his or her term, not having been reelected for the next term

lariat   long rope with a loop at the end, used for catching cattle or horses

legislative branch   law-making branch of the government

lobby   group of people who conduct a campaign to influence lawmakers to vote according to that group's special interests

migrant workers   farm workers who move to various areas as needed

mobile home   vehicle that serves as a house and can be moved by a car or a truck

muckraker   journalist who exposes political corruption

nominate   choose someone to be a candidate

nullify   take away the force of a law, so that it is no longer in effect

paleface   old American-Indian name for a white person

par, at par, up to par   at the level it should be; up to standard

peace pipe   pipe smoked by American Indians as a sign of peace-making

pony express   a system of rapid carrying of mail by relays of horsemen (in the West, about 1860)

pressure group   group that tries to protect or advance its interests by influencing legislative bodies

prospecting   searching an area in hope of finding gold or some other precious material

pull (*noun*)   influence with people who can grant favors

rabbit's foot   the foot of a rabbit, carried for good luck

racket   an organized illegal activity or scheme

ration   a fixed allowance of a scarce product for fair distribution

rat race   violently competitive work or position

rave (about something)   be very enthusiastic; praise excessively

recession   a less drastic form of economic depression (see *depression*)

riding high   being successful and proud

ritzy   elegantly expensive

rodeo   a show exhibiting cowboy skills

rubberneck   one who strains to stare, particularly a rustic impressed by the big city

rubber-stamp (*verb*)   to approve without thinking independently

sandlot   a vacant lot of ground used for playing games; adjective referring to an inexperienced team

scab   a worker who acts against a labor union by working during a strike

segregation   separation because of race difference (or for other reasons); *desegregation* is the correction of this condition

sharecropper   a tenant farmer who pays his or her landlord in farm products

shyster   a lawyer who uses dishonest methods

slapstick   rough comedy

slot machine   a machine for selling or for gambling, operated by putting in money

smart aleck   conceited, arrogant person; a ''wise guy''

square dance   folk dance, with couples arranged in a square

square deal   fair, honest arrangement

squatter   a settler who occupies land that he or she does not own

stump   make campaign speeches to win votes

stump the experts   puzzle or confuse the specialists

sucker   one who is easily taken advantage of

sweatshop   a factory employing workers at low wages, long hours, or other bad conditions

tariff   tax on goods coming into a country

trailer   a vehicle pulled by another vehicle; a mobile home

Uncle Sam   a colloquial name for the United States government

Uncle Tom   a character from the book *Uncle Tom's Cabin*. The name is often used to refer to a black who tries to please or imitate whites.

up-to-date   modern, current, not old-fashioned or outdated

V.I.P.   (colloquial) very important person, given special attention

veto   rejection of legislation by the chief executive of a government (president, governor, mayor)

welfare   financial help from the government to individuals or families in need

wetback   (colloquial) Mexican laborer who entered the United States illegally

whitewash   cover up wrongdoing or crime; make it seem not to be bad

Yankee   person of the northeastern or New England states of the United States

Who? What? Where?

Abolitionist one who favored the abolition of slavery in the United States

AFL-CIO American Federation of Labor and Congress of Industrial Organizations, a combined group of unions including most of the unionized workers in the United States

antipoverty programs government programs to help the poor to become economically independent or to reduce poverty and its evil effects

antitrust laws laws to restrain large combinations of business in order to limit or prevent monopoly and encourage competition

Appalachian Mountains the mountain range in eastern North America, extending from Quebec to Alabama

astronaut explorer who travels beyond the Earth's atmosphere

P.T. Barnum a nineteenth century circus owner who became famous both for his huge tent-circus, which traveled around the country, and for his sarcastic sayings

Bill of Rights the first ten amendments to the U.S. Constitution, a statement of freedoms and rights of individuals

Daniel Boone (see chapter 14)

Boston Tea Party a raid on British ships in Boston Harbor in 1773, in which some disguised Bostonians dumped the cargo of tea into the harbor in protest against the new tea tax

Boy Scouts an organization founded in England in 1908 and widespread in the United States to develop character and self-reliance in its members

Buffalo Bill (Cody) a famous hunter who supplied the teams of railroad builders with buffalo meat in the 1860s

Paul Bunyan a mythical lumberjack. There are many legends about his tremendous size and his remarkable adventures.

Cajuns descendants of French Acadians from Nova Scotia, Canada, who live in Louisiana

Chautauqua annual summer program for the cultural development of working adults—founded at Lake Chautauqua, New York, in 1874. Later, traveling Chautauquas brought "culture" to many rural communities in the U.S.

Chicano a Mexican-American

Civil War (1861–1865) war fought between the southern states, which had broken away from the Union, and the North, which remained faithful to the United States federal government

Colonial period the time from the earliest British settlement in America until the Revolutionary War in 1775

Confederacy   the southern states that fought against the Union in the Civil War

Congress   the federal (national) legislative body of the United States, composed of the Senate and the House of Representatives

Constitution   basic plan of government written by delegates from the states to the Constitutional Convention, which met in Philadelphia in 1787

Creole   a person of the Louisiana region, of French or Spanish ancestry; or, a colonial dialect of French or of another language

Declaration of Independence   the official document (adopted by the Second Continental Congress, July 4, 1776) which declared the rebelling colonies to be "free and independent states" (see chapter 6)

Dixie (or **Dixieland**)   the southeastern states of the United States, especially those of the Confederacy during the Civil War

draft   a system of selecting individuals for compulsory military service, used in the United States (under the name "Selective Service") until it was discontinued in favor of a volunteer army

Emancipation Proclamation   statement by President Abraham Lincoln on January 1, 1863, freeing all the slaves in the areas that were still in rebellion against the Union

Everglades   low, swampy lands with many streams; particularly the Florida Everglades

F.B.I.   Federal Bureau of Investigation, a federal agency that carries out investigations for the Attorney General

federal government   the central or national government of the United States (not state or local government)

Federal Reserve System   the federal banking system of the United States, which exerts much control over credit and the flow of money in the country

Ford Foundation   (see chapter 28)

Girl Scouts   an organization for girls founded in the United States in 1912 to develop citizenship, character, and other valuable qualities in its members

governor   the executive head of a state, elected by the citizens of that state

G.O.P.   the Republican Party (abbreviation for Grand Old Party)

Great Lakes   a series of five very large lakes that make up part of the United States–Canada border

House of Representatives   the lower body of the United States Congress, made up of 435 representatives, each elected by the people of a certain area within a state

impeachment   charges brought against a president, vice-president, or another government official, leading to removal from his position if he is found guilty

Johnny Appleseed   a pioneer fruit grower of the early 1800s. A legend developed that he traveled around the country, sowing apple seeds everywhere.

Ku Klux Klan   a secret, illegal organization in the South, active for some years after the Civil War, opposing the new rights of blacks. (A new group with similar purposes arose in 1915 and has even spread to other parts of the country.)

land grant college   a college or university supported by the federal government in accordance with the Morrill Act (see chapter 24)

Latin America   Central and South America and many of the Caribbean Islands (where Spanish or Portugese is spoken)

Lewis and Clark leaders of an expedition sent out by the United States government right after the Louisiana Purchase (see below) to seek a water route to the North Pacific coast and to make scientific observations of the vast area west of the Mississippi River

Liberty Bell the bell rung (in Independence Hall, Philadelphia) on July 4, 1776, to mark the signing of the Declaration of Independence, now considered a monument of liberty

Louisiana Purchase land bought by the U.S. from France in 1803 for $15,000,000; it extended from the Mississippi to the Rocky Mountains and from the Gulf of Mexico to Canada. This purchase doubled the size of the United States.

Mason-Dixon Line boundary between Pennsylvania and Maryland (named after the surveyors who set the line in the 1760s), which was the border between slave states and free states in eastern United States

Mayflower the sailing ship on which the Pilgrims came to America, landing at Plymouth Rock in Massachusetts

Medicare a national health insurance plan of the United States government for people aged sixty-five or more

Middle West (Midwest) the area from the Ohio River westward to the Rocky Mountains; the north central states of the United States

Minutemen a group of rebellious Colonial American patriots who kept themselves in readiness to fight the British just before and during the Revolutionary War

Mississippi the principal river of the United States. It flows south from northern Minnesota to the Gulf of Mexico.

Monroe Doctrine a declaration by the President of the United States in the early nineteenth century, warning the European powers not to interfere with the newly independent countries of Central and South America

Mormons members of the Church of Jesus Christ of the Latter Day Saints. This sect was founded in New York in the early nineteenth century and later moved to Utah.

National Guard military forces of the various states; it also acts as one of the reserve sections of the U.S. Army

New Deal the program and administration of President Franklin D. Roosevelt

New England general name for the northeastern states, south to, but not including, New York

Nisei American-born person of Japanese ancestry; second generation Japanese-American

Oregon Trail route used in the mid-nineteenth century for migrating westward from Missouri to Oregon

Panama Canal an American-built canal, cutting through the Isthmus of Panama, enabling ships to cross over between the Atlantic and Pacific Ocean, thus linking the east and west coasts of the United States

Pan Americanism the movement to maintain close cooperation among the countries of North, Central, and South America

Pennsylvania Dutch descendants of eighteenth-century German settlers in eastern Pennsylvania. They observe special customs and speak a dialect of German. Most of them are farmers.

Pocahontas   an American Indian girl who is supposed to have saved the life of a leader of the Virginia colony, Captain John Smith, in the early seventeenth century

primary election   election to nominate candidates for various political offices. These candidates will later compete against each other in the general election.

Prohibition   the outlawing of intoxicating liquor in the United States, which was begun in 1919 by the Eighteenth Amendment to the Constitution and repealed in 1933 by the Twenty-first Amendment

Puritans   a strict sect founded in England in the sixteenth century. Massachusetts was settled by Puritans in the seventeenth century.

Reconstruction   the period right after the Civil War when the former Confederate states were reorganized and made ready to re-enter the Union

Paul Revere   an American patriot credited with warning the Massachusetts farmers in his famous midnight ride in 1775 that the British soldiers were approaching

Revolutionary War   the war between England and its thirteen American colonies (1775–1783), which led to the founding of the independent United States

Rockefeller foundations   (see chapter 28)

Rocky Mountains   a high mountain range extending from Alaska to New Mexico in the western part of North America

Betsy Ross   a Philadelphia seamstress who made the first United States flag

Franklin D. Roosevelt   president of the United States during World War II, the only president who ever served in that office for more than two terms

Senate   the upper chamber of the Congress, made up of two senators elected from each state

Social Security   a life-insurance and old-age pension plan maintained by the United States government through compulsory payment by employers and employees

Supreme Court   the highest court of the United States, and head of the federal court system, made up of nine justices

T.V.A.   Tennessee Valley Authority, established in 1933 to develop the Tennessee River area in many ways: building dams to produce electricity; promoting flood control, irrigation, and navigation

Mark Twain   the pen name of Samuel Clemens, a great American writer and humorist of the nineteenth century

Uncle Tom's Cabin   famous novel by Harriet Beecher Stowe that aroused people against slavery

Underground Railroad   (see chapter 11)

Union   the part of the United States that remained loyal to the federal government in the Civil War

Rip Van Winkle   a character (in an early American novel) who slept for twenty years, missing the Revolutionary War

Wall Street   the financial district of New York City, one of the world's most important financial centers

War Between the States   another name for the Civil War; used especially in the South

Wild West   the western frontier in the days before stable government was established in those areas, when some people took the law into their own hands

Williamsburg   the capital of colonial Virginia, which has been restored to its original appearance and is now visited by many tourists

Woodrow Wilson   president of the United States during World War I and chief author and promoter of the League of Nations